Higher Education and the American Dream

Higher Education
and the American Dream

Success and its Discontents

Marvin Lazerson

C E U PRESS

Central European University Press
Budapest—New York

Published in 2010 by
Central European University Press

An imprint of the
Central European University Share Company
Nádor utca 11, H-1051 Budapest, Hungary
Tel: +36-1-327-3138 or 327-3000
Fax: +36-1-327-3183
E-mail: ceupress@ceu.hu
Website: www.ceupress.com

400 West 59th Street, New York NY 10019, USA
Tel: +1-212-547-6932
Fax: +1-646-557-2416
E-mail: mgreenwald@sorosny.org

ISBN 978-963-9776-79-1 cloth

Library of Congress Cataloging-in-Publication Data
Lazerson, Marvin.
Higher education and the American dream : success and its discontents /
Marvin Lazerson.
    p. cm.
Includes bibliographical references and index.
ISBN 978-9639776791 (hardbound)
    1. Education, Higher—United States. 2. Educational change—United
    States. 3. American Dream. I. Title.

LA227.4.L39 2010
378.73—dc22
                                        2010011583

Printed in the USA

This book is dedicated to:

W. Norton Grubb, whose brilliance, passion, and friendship have inspired me for 40 years;

Ursula Wagener, who taught me how to climb mountains, take risks, and understand the meaning of companionship; and

Joshua Lazerson, my grandson, who is a joy and who I hope will understand how valuable an education can be.

Table of Contents

Acknowledgments

The publication of this book by Central European University Press is a measure of my admiration for CEU. The University's goals of intellectual rigor and passionate commitment to democratic societies in a genuinely international environment make it a model of what higher education can be about.

Patricia A. Graham and Yehuda Elkana joined together to invite me to become a faculty member at CEU just as I was preparing to leave the University of Pennsylvania and I am deeply thankful they did. My colleagues in higher education—Livui Matei, Rosita Bateson, and Sophie Howlett—challenged me to expand my knowledge beyond the United States, while Public Policy Department chairs, Uwe Puetter and Nikolai Sittler, asked me to think about public policy in new ways. CEU's President and Rector, John Shattuck, has continued to make the University a welcoming and innovative institution.

I want to thank the staff at CEU for providing a working environment filled with ideas, humor, and skills: Andrea Katalin Csele, Pusa Nastase, Zsuzsanna Szunyogh, Szilvia Kardos, Heni Griecs, Gabriella Kelemen, Klára Papp, and Anikó Hegedűs. At CEU Press, Krisztina Kós oversaw the process of converting a manuscript into a book with professional skill and Parker Snyder made the text eminently readable.

Early versions of individual chapters appeared in *Annals of the American Academy of Political and Social Science, Change: the Magazine of Higher Education, Chronicle of Higher Education,* and *Education Week.*

Introduction:
Houses, Automobiles, and Higher Education

See the USA in your Chevrolet
America is asking you to call
Drive your Chevrolet through the USA
America's the greatest land of all
(Sung by Dinah Shore in a 1952 television advertisement)

The university has eliminated more than 500 jobs, including deans, department chairmen and hundreds of teaching assistants. Last month Mr. Crow [the university president] announced that the university would close 48 programs, cap enrollment and move up the freshman application deadline by five months. Every employee, from Mr. Crow down, will have 10–15 days unpaid furlough this spring.

(*New York Times*, March 17, 2009)

This is a story of success, unbelievable success, and of the discontents that came with it. Higher education in the United States has been the victim of its own success. As it became the only route to an increasing number of professions and the primary path to economic success, it generated higher and higher expectations, an enormous expansion of enrollments, and money. With these, came discontent and disappointments.

During the last half of the 20th century higher education in the United States triumphed. Few industries grew as fast, or gained such prestige, or affected the lives of so many people. Higher education received remarkable sums of money from federal, state, and local governments. Alumni and foundations gave generously to it. Families reached into their savings, postponed purchases, and went into debt so that their children could go to college. Higher education, even more than elementary and secondary schools, simultaneously embodied both a public good and a private benefit. It served public purposes beneficial to the nation's economy, protected the national defense, opened up new avenues of knowledge, developed new technologies, and made palpable the goal of equality of educational opportunity. It provided extraordinary private benefits such that individuals who possessed it improved their access to higher income, status, and security. Along with purchasing a house and buying a new automobile, it was a pillar of the American dream.

For me that dream was real. In 1948 my parents, grandfather, baby sister and I moved from a crowded apartment in New York City to a one-square-mile unincorporated village called Carle Place on Long Island, just outside the city. Our house was built by William Levitt, who took advantage of new technologies and factory-like production processes and guaranteed loans to builders given by the Federal Housing Administration, and low-interest mortgages provided by the Veterans Administration, to create inexpensive tract housing for people like my parents. Although such housing, spreading across the American landscape, would be lampooned—called "little boxes" filled with oppressively conformist people in the song made famous by folksinger Pete Seeger—the critics missed the essential point. Having one's own house was a dream come true.

Levitt also made clear how intertwined the country's automobile industry was to the housing industry, once comparing himself to General Motors. The connection was reaffirmed by the *New York Times* (February 6, 1994) in an article entitled, "How William Levitt Helped to Fulfill the American Dream," suggesting that Henry Ford and William Levitt were part of an American package. Such esoteric understandings were not a feature of my parents' repertoire, and I was too young to realize the cultural significance. But I did recognize that something special had happened when my father arrived home one day in the mid-1950s in a brand new, two-tone Oldsmobile, a car which became my parents' most prized possession and the one which I drove on my first high school dates. Federally financed highways, low cost gasoline, and technological innovations combined with federally financed home building, low interest mortgages, and new technologies to give my family two of the pillars of the American Dream.

If the house and automobile were the first signs of a dream come true, they soon gave way to the greatest aspiration of all: sending the kids to college. Although I recognized that my mother's return to the labor market while I was in high school had something to do with our education, I never quite understood how my parents could send my sister, Shelly, and I to private universities in New York and Boston. To this day, it remains a mystery how they did it, but I knew that their dream, to say nothing of my sister's and mine, was our higher education. Houses and automobiles could come and go; a college degree was permanent, and a statement: Our family had made it in America.

By the time I went to college, *Brown v. Board of Education* (1954) had been decided, the civil rights movement was underway and I recognized what millions of African Americans had always known— the American Dream was considerably less real for some than for others; housing, automobiles, and higher education were inequitably distributed. Many got them, but many were also being denied them. The civil rights movement took aim at each of those. As the Great Society took shape in the late 1960s, the broad sweep of the movement continued, but it was also clear that education had become the central focus. Whatever could be done to correct inequities was appropriate, but over time public policy came to focus on the education pillar of the American Dream, a phenomenon that would be reinforced by the women's movement.

By the last decades of the 20th century higher education had achieved a virtual monopoly on middle class and professional status. Universities and colleges became the licensing agency for Americans who wanted to enter the professions. Every occupation sought to increase its prestige and income by making a college degree (and beyond) the requirement for entry. For countless Americans, going to college was the route upward and they expected their governments at every level to help make that happen, especially through grants and loans to students, branch campuses of the state university, and through local community colleges. Even when growing income returns to higher education slowed or plateaued during the 1970s and 1980s and the costs of attending college escalated, going to college remained the dream. As the job market for those without college deteriorated into dead end jobs at fast food franchises, continuing one's education became a necessity to keep from losing out in the economic race. Families and students, in increasing numbers older students, dug into their savings and took out loans in order to attend.

Higher education, however, became a victim of its own success, bringing criticism, controversy, and doubt. The seemingly unstoppable demand to attend college and university, the availability of government and private money to do so, and the desire within every state and local community to have its own college or university, made it easy for higher education to charge what the traffic would bear. By the 1980s, those costs so substantially outpaced inflation and the growth rate of median family income that higher education looked like yet another greedy industry. The 1990s brought renewed inflows of money and an ideology of being more market-oriented, becoming in effect like the other industries in America, leading to the view that things would just keep on getting better and better. Institutions with endowments and large sums of money could invest and receive double-digit returns; institutions with little in the way of surplus income simply acted as if they too would join the league of the rich, if only they had the right investment advisor. It was just going to get better and better. The dot-com bubble burst around 2000, but memories of the bust dimmed quickly, until 2008 and 2009 arrived with devastating financial consequences. It turned out that the higher education industry was in fact little different than the housing and automobile industries. The same ethos that had fueled housing and large automobiles had also fueled higher education.

Higher education's emergence as a giant industry affected almost every aspect of its organizational structures, including its professors. In the decades after World War II professors gained enormous public stature and a presence once barely imaginable. The stereotypes of absentminded, befuddled professors disappeared, replaced by a growing number of government advisors, policy analysts, and corporation consultants, writing best selling books, newspaper articles and regularly appearing as public intellectuals on television. An academic revolution occurred, to use Christopher Jencks and David Riesman's term (1968), with professors gaining authority over hiring and promotion, curriculum and teaching, and, for those who brought in external funds for research, becoming free agents in the job market. The canons of shared governance, which held until the 1980s, meant that faculty members made things happen. Professors attached their primary allegiances to the academic disciplines; success at gaining funding for their research became the route to stature and power. Once primarily responsible for teaching undergraduate survey courses, general education, and relatively simple versions of their academic disciplines, professors at the highest status institutions made graduate education their primary interest.

These changes occurred neither everywhere nor to the same degree. Research and external funding played a lesser role outside research universities. At liberal arts colleges, at the comprehensive state universities that were not centers of research, and at the growing number of community colleges, undergraduate teaching remained the primary responsibility. Occasionally long-reigning autocratic presidents could run roughshod over faculty, and public officials could certainly make life difficult. Still, in comparison to the past, the new authority of the professoriate and their academic disciplines set the terms of status, power, and identity. Rarely did professors call themselves teachers. They were physicists, historians, linguists, and economists. Administrators everywhere routinely articulated the basic principle of the academic revolution: the faculty was the heart of the institution.

That is, until the 1980s when such words had a hollow ring, for by then a new ethos of higher education had established itself, one that grew evermore exaggerated and powerful—the ethos of the market. Although a market orientation, the selling and buying of higher education and its products, had always existed—19th century college presidents, for example, regularly did the rounds seeking funds and students and the curriculum was always being adjusted to attract students—the market as the compelling force took on a whole new *gravitas* at the end of the 20th century. And with it, an enormous shift in the balance of power in higher education occurred. Institutional managers proliferated and grew more powerful. They became the primary institutional sellers, were responsible for managing the extraordinary amounts of money that flowed into higher education, set the terms for campus growth, and handled human resources and public relations. Governing boards took on more power. Since most board members came from the world of money, at least the most influential of them, they understood the most important attributes of the market and thus possessed the most important knowledge. Students brought two basic ingredients to the mix: money and brains. Their ever increasing tuition payments balanced budgets; their brains brought prestige, as the relationship between entering students SAT scores and graduation rates attested to a given school's institutional ranking. In return students expected to be treated as well-served customers and assumed that their degrees would be valuable when they entered the labor market. Faculty, once the most important decisions makers, lost power. They held onto things like faculty appointments, but the truly big decisions, like where institutional resources would go, whether to biology or history or to a newcomer like public policy, or to student services or graduate student fellowships, were not faculty-made decisions. And, as the proportion of part-time instructors grew, so too did the divisiveness within faculty ranks.

The professoriate's success in making research the mark of status meant their connection to teaching withered. As they became prominent advisors and consultants, they became caught up in political conflicts, as in the role of the "best and the brightest" during the Vietnam War, in the contestations over civil rights, and in their prominence in the federal government. As the costs of college increased, as downsizing and restructuring hit American industry, and as public subsidies came under fire, professors' responsibilities came into question. The academic freedom professors had gained became caught up in the snares of political correctness and the entitlements of tenure. Could they really never be fired? Did they only teach 12 hours a week? Questions like these were the public face of growing discontent. The academic disciplines themselves, which had been the heart of the academy, came to look like walls against new approaches to learning; the power of academic departments seemed to serve mainly to undermine decisions taken in the interest of the college or university as a whole. A widespread joke with much truth attached to it circulated: The faculty voted 75 percent to 25 percent for the reform measure, so it failed. Professors could easily be lampooned for always standing against change. The mega size of the higher education industry and the high expectations that surrounded it made higher education an easy target for media and political criticism.

As the 21st century began, higher education looked like other powerful industries. There was indeed a remarkable resemblance between higher education and the U.S. automobile industry. The latter had achieved an importance in post World War II America based on its technical superiority, astute marketing, diligence in providing customers what they thought they wanted—large and powerful autos with numerous models and sleek looking designs—regularly adding new essentials, whether power windows, V8 engines, air conditioning, mini-vans, four-wheel drive, SUVs, and always more room for the family. Like the higher education industry, it sold itself as a pillar of the American dream.

There were of course discontents, irritants directed toward the automobile industry. Small and better made cars from Japan emerged as threatening competitors. U.S. auto makers countered with a few small cars of their own, but the fact was small cars were not big money makers, and therefore never really taken seriously. Ralph Nader, a harsh critic, threatened the industry when he discovered that General Motors' Corvair, with its rear engine, would upend while driving, but the Corvair quickly disappeared from the market and Nader was relabeled as a nut. Sporadic government efforts to require more fuel-efficient cars were easily beaten back or watered down. Sure Chrysler needed a government bailout, but that was a minor investment next to the decades-long federal subsidies of the highway system (and neglect of mass transit), and besides the cost of gasoline remained low.

The higher education industry manifested many of the same characteristics. A barely noticeable industry before World War II, higher education emerged as an American success story, widely admired—though little understood—around the world. Like the automobile industry, it showed itself remarkably deft at marketing and at continually adding new institutions, new programs, and new facilities. When the proportion of college age youth in the population dropped in the early 1980s, leading to dire warnings about the future of higher education, the problem was quickly resolved, as greater proportions of young people elected to go to college (purchase the product and invest in the future) and a whole new market—adult learners and lifelong learning—was created. If new automobiles represented an immediate statement about the American dream, going to college and beyond was an investment in the dream.

As with the automobile industry, higher education had its discontents. Conservatives condemned the civil rights and anti-Vietnam War demonstrations on college campuses during the 1960s and 1970s. Then Governor of California Ronald Reagan used this souring mood toward higher education to reduce the University of California at Berkeley, perhaps the greatest public university the U.S. has ever had, to a shadow of its former self. Affirmative action programs, which opened places to women and minorities became targets of attack, claiming they badly lowered the quality of students and faculty, as well as being discriminatory of white males. The federal government changed its financial aid policy from grants to student loans, making it harder for those of modest means to attend. Always there was worry that for all the opportunities provided by colleges and universities, too much of higher education replicated existing social class structures. But while these and other irritants made the situation more difficult for higher education, as similar ones did for the automobile industry, they did not alter the fundamental fact that students kept coming in search of the American dream.

In the first decade of the 21st century the automobile industry collapsed, along with the housing market, two of the pillars of success in America. The weight of their failures simply became too great: greed, callous indifference to the environment, and a failure to take foreign competition seriously, combining with the virtual disappearance of easy credit. The higher education system did not collapse, but it faced complaints similar to those of the automobile industry: chastised for offering overpriced, poor-quality products, poor services, inefficient and bureaucratic, unwilling to adapt to new markets, technologically backward, administratively bloated, uninterested in teaching, and more concerned with frills than the core product. The automobile industry may indeed remake itself; Americans have a way of doing that. General Motors claims to be reinventing itself, by being slimmer, more focused on quality, and committed to the environment. The jury will be out for some time. The higher education industry is also in the throes of trying to remake itself. When endowments at the richest universities dropped by 25–30% and gifts declined, the costs of business as usual became too great. All the obvious steps took place: cutting staff and programs, canceling capital investments and delaying maintenance projects, renegotiating debt, holding back increases in salaries and financial aid packages. Such cuts were actually the simplest part and there was little choice. As the financial crisis worked its way through, money has come back into the system. The after shocks remain, however. Deferred maintenance has crippling consequences because the costs tend to escalate over time. The shift to part-time faculty, already underway during the last two decades, is accelerating, and almost no one knows what will be the consequences. The use of cost/profit measurements to decide what should be offered as education or what kind of research should be done, already commonplace by the 1990s, is even more intense, just as equity concerns seem to be diminishing. It is clear that competition within and conflict over higher education is increasing. The fact that more than 45 percent of entering college students fail to graduate, with even higher percentages of minority students and students from low income families, is disheartening. That students are learning much less than they ought is troubling. Technology has made all forms of education less place-bound and more borderless, leading to enormous insecurity as to what the industry is about and even where it is located. If no one really understands where the internet is, then what will happen when educational institutions are simply on the web? Vocationally- and professionally-oriented adult learners have become essential customers of higher education, perhaps even more so than the once traditional age group of 17–22 year-olds, with consequences only beginning to be grasped. The returns to higher education remain high, so the desire to attend will continue, meaning that the selling and buying of higher education is going to intensify. The discontents, however, are not going away.

Marvin Lazerson
Rottach-Egern, Germany–Budapest, Hungary

Part I

The Gospel of Getting Ahead

CHAPTER 1

Building the dream (and worrying about it)

If you build it, he will come.
(From the 1989 movie *Field of Dreams*)

Has higher education become too successful? That's something of a rhetorical question, given that in the United States Americans like to say, "You can't argue with success." Are the expectations for higher education too grandiose? Absolutely, and therein lies one of the industry's dilemmas.

Higher education has indeed been one of the American wonders. Fueled by aspirations for an educated citizenry and upward mobility through expanded educational opportunities, with aspirations that put more young people into school for longer periods than had ever occurred, education became central to the American way of life. Colleges and universities became part of this phenomenon, with escalating intensity after World War II, propelled by expansive government investments, by growing income returns and greater access to professions, and by regional competition that impelled states and localities to build new campuses and expand existing ones. Higher education quickly changed from its relatively minor role in American life before the middle of the 20th century into a major industry.

Images of absent-minded professors, raccoon coats and fraternities, quiet out-of-the way campuses, of Cary Grant, Mickey Rooney and June Allison, with an occasional Katherine Hepburn to leaven the mix—movie stars of the 1930s, 40s, and 50s—continued in revised form in such movies as *The Absent-Minded Professor* and the alcohol consuming campuses of *Animal House,* images that continued to suggest how frivolous college could be. But these images were also complemented, and to a significant degree replaced, by the reality that in the second half of the 20th century professors were taken to be studious academics interested in research and their laboratories, people who could be seen on television and writing in newspapers commenting on current issues. Their work supported national defense—the research that produced the atom bomb was largely done by professors—their breakthroughs in medical research were astounding, and they became central figures in articulating economic and social policies. Millions of Americans clamored for access to college and their aspirations soon made college entry the stuff of politics, with debates over affirmative action and financial aid taking center stage. The numbers and the money that flowed into higher education were staggering.

In almost every regard, the last half of the 20th century was good for higher education. Three sets of data tell the story of growth: more institutions, increasing enrollments, and more money. Between 1950 and 2000, the number of degree granting institutions more than doubled, from 1,851 to 4,084. Enrollment growth was even more impressive with total enrollment increasing from 2.6 million to 14.8 million students, more than fivefold in the same fifty years. The amount of money was extraordinary. In 2008 dollars, annual expenditures went from $2.2 billion in 1950 to $134.6 billion in 1990 (National Center for Education Statistics, 2008, Table 187), and the amounts kept on growing thereafter. The growth in each of these areas reaffirmed what Americans had come to believe: America was a forward-looking nation, a point of view articulated by the actor Ronald Reagan, soon to become Governor of California and President of the United States, whose television voice in the 1950s and early 1960s told the American people, "At General Electric, progress is our most important product."

Progress was not smooth and the picture was sometimes not so glamorous. Just as American industries—textiles, steel, and automobiles—found themselves threatened by foreign imports and global competition, by managerial miscalculations and worker demands for higher wages, shorter workweeks, and full-coverage medical insurance, so too did higher education find itself troubled. In the immediate postwar period anticommunist mania led to charges that the Reds and their fellow travelers had invaded America's campuses. The Soviet Union's launch of Sputnik in 1957 raised doubts about whether American standards of academic achievement were stringent enough for the Cold War era. Demonstrations, strikes, and violence during the 1960s and early 1970s divided higher education from within, and diminished enthusiasm for it among politicians and the public at large. One version of the criticism was colleges and universities had become yet another mistaken entitlement of the welfare state. A slowdown in income returns to those with a college education during the 1970s combined with the rising costs of going to college—the industry seemed unable or unwilling to rein in its expenditures—opened higher education to even more strident criticism, complemented by efforts to reduce federal and state expenditures. During the 1980s, state appropriations, the largest source of government funds for higher education, increased only slightly per student, in fact, remaining unchanged when measured in constant dollars. Government funding as a percentage of funding for higher education declined during the 1980s. Questioners challenged whether colleges and universities were teaching students anything, whether higher education really added any "value" to the students or whether it just certified them for the labor market. With remedial programs for entering college students proliferating, the notion of "higher education" sometimes sounded like a misnomer. The media joined in with increasing glee, as it found itself yet another institution corrupt in its ways, reporting on the misuse of funds, luxuries for administrators and students, and professors who taught very little and were often jetting off to somewhere else rather than being on campus.

And yet as irritating, threatening, and confusing as these moments were, most times of trouble were transitory. Each rocky moment was followed by renewed enthusiasm, more applications for admission, expansion of facilities, and greater success at raising money. The anti-communist McCarthyism of the 1950s shook some campuses, frightened many faculty, and ruined careers, but it hardly made a dent in the industry's growth or prestige. Sputnik produced considerable criticism and worries, but out of it came the National Defense Education Act of 1958, which gave unprecedented federal fiscal support for the sciences, foreign languages, area studies, and campus growth. A few years later the Higher Education Act of 1965 opened the doors to even more people through a massive program of financial aid for low-income students, part of the growing sense that higher education was critical to national defense and economic growth. The campus rebellions that shocked the nation in the 60s and early 70s led to angry diatribes directed at overly entitled youth, but the public's shifting attitudes toward the civil rights movement and the Vietnam War ultimately gave legitimacy to the demonstrations. Certainly few if any young people turned away from attending college because students had protested. The most obvious direct impact of the student demonstrations was to give students more freedom. Campus restrictions to student life effectively disappeared in the 1970s, as *in loco parentis* became a dirty word. The number of required courses declined and the size of the overall curriculum increased, giving students more choices in what to take and faculty more freedom to teach what they wanted. Income and status returns to college attendance remained high, and if the rate of growth slowed and may have even declined slightly after 1970, attending college was still a wise decision in comparison to not going, as the job market for high school graduates collapsed. With predictions at the beginning of the 1980s that the declining number of 17- to 21-year olds in the population would substantially diminish the market for students, higher education discovered that greater proportions were seeking enrollment and also turned to nontraditional students (more accurately returned to them, since the G. I. Bill after World War II, which provided tuition and living expenses to returning veterans, had brought millions of young adults to the campuses). While it was becoming more difficult for families to pay for their child's college education, as tuition costs rose faster than the rates of inflation and average family income, the numbers scrambling to get into college kept going up. Community colleges in particular burst at the seams enrolling high school graduates and dropouts, adults seeking job preparation, and others simply wanting a place to learn more about the world and themselves. The precipitous drop in the stock market in 1987, which looked like a major threat to the higher education industry, was quickly followed by an incredible run of income returns, making it seem that every college and university with the right investment strategy could be secure, if not rich.

Despite the ups and downs, during the last half of the 20th century, higher education built its field of dreams. One had to let the public know the field was there, market the products, build student-friendly facilities, and create a number of different leagues, from high prestige expensive to low prestige budget institutions, so that everyone had a place to go. Sometimes rain fell and conditions were poor, some teams operated in the red and folded. But like the newly constructed domed stadiums, higher education's field of dreams was a remarkable invention, able to resist all kinds of bad weather. Higher education could take pride in its success.

1.1 Building the dream

The times for higher education were so good that the management guru and social commentator Peter Drucker proclaimed in 1958 that "we cannot get enough educated people. In the past the question had always been, how many educated people can a society afford? Today it is increasingly, how many people who are not highly educated can a society afford?" (Blumberg, 1980, p. 26). In 1992 a historian would simply refer to the two and one-half decades after World War II as "academia's golden age" (Freeland, 1992).

The Servicemen's Readjustment Act of 1944 (the G. I. Bill) and the President's Commission on Higher Education in 1947 (the Truman Commission) set the terms of postwar expansion. Although many Americans had, by the 1930s, come to see college enrollment as an important ingredient of the "culture of aspiration" (Levine, 1986), the veterans' determination to go to college was mind boggling. Under the G. I. Bill, between 1945 and 1949, 2.2 million veterans (overwhelmingly men) enrolled in college and post-secondary institutions, three times more than the maximum projected during the Act's passage. Older than the traditional college students, more explicitly vocationally oriented, and impatient with the traditions of college life, especially since many were married with children, the veterans dramatized and reinforced the inextricable link between getting ahead, grabbing a piece of the American dream, and enrolling in college. At least three consequences emerged from this early post-War success. Although the G. I. Bill was initially seen as a way to keep returning veterans from immediately entering the labor market, and thus flooding it with more job seekers than jobs, the federal grants to support college attendance linked federal largesse to the expansion of educational opportunity—a fact which surprised both the original supporters of the Bill and the higher education community itself, which had been wary of too many of the wrong kinds of students coming. Second, the veterans, older and often with families, were less interested in "college life" and more interested in their studies; they helped make going to college a serious endeavor. And third, the veterans' academic success demolished the traditional idea that only a select few could benefit from college. As a result, a new conception emerged of who and how many should go to college and who would pay for it.

The Report of the President's Commission on Higher Education (1947), significantly titled, *Higher Education for American Democracy*, had no immediate effect on public policy. What it did was to articulate the twin themes that fueled higher education's prosperity. First, it asserted that equality of higher educational opportunity was essential to America's economic growth and national defense. An expansive higher education system with public funding would fulfill simultaneously the possibility that every American would have the opportunity to achieve the American dream while ensuring that the nation would be more prosperous and more secure. This would require active, indeed aggressive, federal involvement and investment in post-secondary education, including free, tax-supported public community colleges. As the Commission wrote, "To meet the needs of the economy our schools must train many more young people for employment as medical secretaries, recreational leaders, hotel and restaurant managers, aviators, salesmen in fields like life insurance and real estate, photographers, automotive and electrical technicians, and...medical technicians, dental hygienists, nurses' aides, laboratory professions" (President's Commission on Higher Education, 1947, vol. I, 68–69). Few had ever spoken so bluntly about public sponsorship of post-secondary education for the labor market. The Commission's prediction that higher education would in the coming decades enroll millions more students and that their explicit focus would be jobs was totally accurate. As America began the 1950s, higher education was about to enter a whole new world.

The G. I. Bill initiated and the 1947 President's Commission on Higher Education blessed the postwar expansion, but the directions higher education took evolved in ground that had already been well-prepared. Over the course of the previous decades, four established

themes combined to lay the foundation for the postwar era: vocationalism, public higher education, multiple sectors of post-secondary schooling, and research. America's appetite for higher education grew out of these earlier developments but with an intensity
that had never before been seen. The battle over vocationalism—
the direct application of schooling to jobs and economic opportunities—for example, had been joined since the 19th century. Seeking
students and public approbation many nineteenth century colleges
adapted their liberal arts traditions to become multipurpose schools,
diversifying their curricula and becoming sensitive to local and
regional economic needs and job opportunities (Geiger, 1995). For
women especially, vocationalism was always central. Overwhelmingly, female students traditionally had prepared for teaching.

Between 1880 and the 1930s, vocationalism took form through
development of professional schools, the creation of an educational
ladder between high school and college, so that there was a structured progression through levels of schooling into the labor market,
and because employers began to rely upon college credentials as a
criterion for hiring. Each of these was important. The appearance of
business schools, engineering, education, social work, nursing, and
dental schools and the growth of law and medical schools pointed
higher education toward direct application to specific occupations.
The creation of an educational ladder that went from elementary
and secondary schools through colleges and universities made the
latter the apex of the educational system, while simultaneously
reducing 19th century competitors, like academies, high schools,
one- and two-year normal schools, private proprietary schools, and
apprenticeships, to institutions that were merely preparatory to college or even of a lesser status. By the 1930s, the high school, which
had once paralleled college, had become its subordinate; increasingly, without a high school degree there was no entry to college
and without a collegiate education, no entry to graduate schools.
Entry into professions meant extended schooling.

The shift in the criteria for employment was generated in part by
the growth of white collar jobs within corporate and public agencies
and by the expansion of professional occupations, which seemed
ideally suited for the kinds of learning and socialization that occurred
at college. This generated much of the consumer-driven growth in

post-secondary enrollments before World War II, much of which was connected to a large number of part-time young adults enrolled in professional degree programs in America's cities. Still, the movement of young people into higher education before World War II was hardly massive, especially since large numbers of youth left high school without graduating to enter the labor market. The foundations of post-World War II expansion, however, had been laid. Going to college rather than not going meant greater returns to income and professional status. That was a phenomenon the veterans of World War II recognized before anyone else.

A second critical ingredient of postwar expansion had also been put in place earlier, the growth of the public sector in higher education. Although Americans tend to associate public higher education with the post World War II period, large proportions of young people had always attended publicly supported colleges and universities. The Morrill Acts of 1862 and 1890, provided federal support for state universities, and furthered the notion that higher education was a public responsibility, a mechanism for developing national and regional economies. Individuals might gain from going to college, but the primary gain was to the public good. Whatever the obvious differences between elementary/secondary schooling and college, an argument was well-established before World War II that all levels of education enhanced the social and economic needs of the nation, state, and locality, and thus deserved public support.

The third critical ingredient of postwar expansionism was the organizational forms that had been previously established, principally decentralization and differentiation. Because higher education was always a decentralized industry, made up of relatively autonomous institutions competing within a deregulated market, it expanded in whatever ways it thought necessary or could find support. Often this meant changing admissions requirements to attract more students (or, in a few cases, to become more selective), providing fiscal incentives to students to attend, revising the curriculum to make it more attractive, expanding student life activities, and seeking funding from alumni and philanthropists. Higher education had thus established its entrepreneurial orientation well before the mid-twentieth century. Added to this was the existence of segmented and differentiated institutions. Higher education accepted the equation that access to college could be widespread if the system was segmented. A complex web of different kinds of post-secondary institutions was already in place by the late 1930s: including junior and community colleges that provided one to two years of schooling to anyone who chose to come, normal schools for future teachers (almost all women) that required varying lengths of time, state universities available to residents, a small number of selective liberal arts colleges, and large research universities. The variation and the gradients of status increased opportunities for students while allowing individual institutions to choose their admissions requirements, although this was something of a non-event since many colleges and universities desperately needed students anyway. American higher education could thus claim—rightly—that it provided widespread opportunities for many, and was meritocratic. The combination seemed irresistibly compelling.

The fourth strand in the pre-World War II era that later proved potent was the "research university." The American research university took shape in the last decades of the 19th century drawing upon German antecedents. With the founding of new institutions, like Johns Hopkins University, the University of Chicago, and Cornell University, and the remaking of older institutions like Harvard, Columbia, and the University of Pennsylvania, American higher education began to take on the mantle of research as its defining ethos. In part, this reflected a controversial shift in what higher education stood for, a movement from responsibility to transmit existing knowledge to students through teaching to taking on responsibility for discovering new knowledge. The former required an informed teacher who told students what was known; the latter required professors who understood how to discover the unknown, and to transmit that to more sophisticated students so that they too could engage in the act of discovery. The emergent research orientation required not simply classrooms, but laboratories, archives for the collection of primary documents, and scientific rigor. The shift toward a research orientation involved a belief that ultimately research, particularly in the natural sciences and social sciences, would find applications, something that the experiences of World War I suggested would occur. Although the research enterprise remained a modest feature of higher education before 1940—indeed, most professors have never been highly active researchers—the successes and structure of research that had evolved received a tremendous boost during World War II, and American higher education entered the last half of the 20th century ready to give luster to research and receive money far beyond what anyone could have imagined.

With the war's end, Americans built upon the organizational forms, vocational expectations, public commitments, and research agendas to accelerate the expansion of their higher education system. The veterans' response to the G. I. Bill showed just how effective the prewar developments had been; the Truman Commission gave voice to the expansive behavior of the veterans, pushing the ideology of higher educational opportunity further than it had ever previously gone. Higher education was organized so that all kinds of students could go to all kinds of places. Research had established its value. Few truly understood it at the time, but the rush for places and money was on.

1.2 Why did they come?

Why higher education expanded and why students went to college have been the subject of countless interpretations. The most commonly held view of why the system expanded—and one that remains the most prominent explanation (Goldin and Katz, 2008)—is that the modernization of American society, especially its adoption of advanced technologies, made education more important. Governments and corporations invested in it because it would pay off. During most of the 20th century, the United States was at the forefront in the uses of sophisticated technology and thus the demand for education increased, with gains for the economy and for the individual. The downside of these developments was that those with less education were less likely to benefit from economic growth. In this human capital model—nowadays commonly referred to as the Knowledge Society or the Knowledge Economy—an economy that depends upon technological growth requires individuals with sufficiently advanced education both to invent the technology and to take full advantage of it. Those individuals with the appropriate technical and literacy skills are worth more in the marketplace because they are more productive and effectively make greater contributions to the national economy. The gains to increasing participation in advanced education were thus three-fold: educated people contributed more to the economy; they received greater fiscal rewards and greater prestige for doing so; and higher education itself grew at rapid rates. Almost every discussion of the need for a mass-producing higher education system repeated and continues to repeat these arguments. This has had the effect of making higher education a central driver of economic growth and the path to the American dream of success. As Goldin and Katz (2008, p. 41) conclude: "Human capital, embodied in one's people, is the most fundamental part of the wealth of nations. Other inputs, such as natural resources and financial capital, can be acquired at world prices in global markets, but the efficiency of one's labor force rarely can be. Not only does more education make the labor force more efficient, it makes people better able to embrace all kinds of change including the introduction of new technologies. And, for some extraordinary individuals, more education enables them to create new technologies."

Although the human capital interpretation of the growth of higher education remains the most common, it is not the only interpretation. An alternative view of expansionism is less positive: higher education expanded in a segmented and hierarchical fashion in ways that preserved the social structure of inequality. This was an artful process in which those with more to start their lives—in terms of monetary, social, and cultural capital—gained more than those who did not. Individuals went to those colleges that roughly paralleled the social class from which they came and, if they experienced some upward mobility, the overall effect was to leave the nation as socially divided as in the past. In particular, the lengthening of educational requirements for jobs, with increasing numbers of professional jobs requiring schooling beyond the bachelor's degree, made it easier for those who could afford to stay in school longer to rise to the top of the occupational hierarchy. Almost every advocate of the shift toward a greater emphasis on more open admissions, affirmative action, greater commitment to remedial programs, and the priority of equity draws upon this interpretation, calling for public policies that break the system's tendency to replicate the social class structure.

A third interpretation has focused on the way credentialing served to accentuate the expansion of educational opportunity. This view suggests that higher education provided a cultural currency that status-driven employers found especially attractive, less because of the technical skills learned in college (the human capital model), than because of the organizational and behavioral attributes necessary to be successful in college and because the existence or nonexistence of a degree was easily measurable. The college degree was a credential that certified a modest level of knowledge and literacy, but also certified the kind of person who could work within a complex organization or as a professional. In that sense, higher education is more a signal or symbol than a concrete contribution to real life productive skills.

These interpretations are not mutually exclusive, and in fact all have been at work over time. All in some measure are oversimplifications of complex processes that are themselves very hard to measure. Indeed, a modest scholarly industry has sprung up in order to ascertain what higher education adds or does not add to the economy and returns to individuals. In addition, this industry has been active in trying to determine what are the indirect returns to higher education—the social and personal skills gained by individuals (including their contributions to social life via, e.g., learned levels of tolerance), as well as the indirect payoffs in terms of job provisions in areas surrounding colleges and universities. Every time a governor or state legislature suggests that the public investment in higher education is too high, institutions immediately produce long reports showing how important they are to the state and local economies.

The answer to the central question of "why did individuals go to college" is that they saw the issue in relatively simple terms: they believed and continue to believe that it paid to go to college. And, in broad terms with numerous caveats they were right. Large numbers of Americans were and remain willing to pay substantial fees, borrow large sums of money, and support public subsidies to higher education because they are convinced that it is in their best interest, including believing that higher education furthers national defense, economic growth, and equality of educational opportunity. As Grubb and Lazerson (2004, p. 161) conclude: "formal schooling increases earnings, protects individuals from the effects of inflation, and increases earnings by more than the costs involved." Or, as Goldin and Katz (2008, p. 325) put it, "education is still a very good investment. In fact the marginal individual who does not graduate high school, who does not continue to college, and who does not complete college, is leaving large amounts of money lying on the street." Students and their families who realize that going to college brings better jobs, higher income, professional status, and greater security are reading the labor market correctly.

Still, if the overall story is that it has and continues to pay to go to college and beyond, the caveats are numerous and not widely understood, with the result that the individual benefits have often been exaggerated, "leading to disappointments and a suspicion of formal schooling when its promises are not realized—for example, when cyclical variation in demand leaves well-educated engineers or computer programmers unemployed, or when college students fail to find high-status employment after graduating and wind up driving taxis or working in restaurants, or when training does not increase earnings as promised. Higher levels of schooling cannot guarantee access to better employment and higher earnings; they may be necessary, but they are often not sufficient" (Grubb and Lazerson, 2004, Ch. 6).

More detailed examinations of the income returns to college attendance reveal, for example, that substantial variations exist by fields of study, by gender, and by race. "Among two-year [community college] associate degrees, only those in business, engineering-and computer-related fields, and health (dominated by nursing) are substantially more valuable than others, while those in education (largely child care), public service (like fire and police protection), and various craft occupations yield no greater benefits than a high school degree. At the baccalaureate level, these differences become even clearer: graduates in engineering and health enjoy the highest benefits, followed by business and science/mathematics majors: those with degrees in the humanities, the social sciences, and education rank at the bottom" (Grubb and Lazerson, 2004, p. 161). The differences by field of study become even greater at the post-baccalaureate level. Graduate degrees in law, medicine, engineering, and business pay substantially more than do those in education and social welfare.

When one adds gender and race to the mixture, the portrait related to fields of study changes, since both women and underrepresented racial minorities have benefited relatively even more than white males from the expansion of higher education opportunity. Under the impact of the women's movement, rates of enrollment for women soared beginning with the cohort of women born in the 1960s, who by the early 21st century comprised 56 percent of all undergraduate students (Goldin and Katz, 2008, pp. 251–253). Income returns to women grew substantially compared to men. Levy and Murnane (1992, pp. 1355–1357) found that between 1979 and 1987, there was an "eight percent increase in the median earnings of 25–34 year old male college graduates" but a "21 percent increase in the median earnings of 25–34 old female college graduates." Racial and ethnic minorities continue to lag behind whites in participation rates and income returns—although it is significant that minority enrollments have grown dramatically in the last half century and the proportional financial gain to minority students, especially minority women who complete college, is higher than it is for whites. Still the differences remain disturbing. While about 40 percent of the white college-age cohort attend college, around 30 percent of blacks and some 25 percent of Hispanics attend. Perhaps even more telling, whites graduate in higher proportions than do minorities, and minorities are considerably more likely to be enrolled in community colleges (Altbach, Reisberg, and Rumbly, 2009, pp. 41–42).

Added to this is the disturbing phenomenon, found by McPherson, Bowen, and Chingos (2009). Using data drawn from students entering four-year colleges in 2003, they found that only 56 percent graduated. Minority students graduate at even lower rates, as do students from low income families. If one were to put community college students completing two-year degrees, the proportions would be much worse. And this comes at a time when income returns to getting a college degree have been rising.

These challenges to the American dream of "go to college, get a better job" are serious, in the sense that they reveal how far Americans have to go to achieve a genuine equality of educational opportunity. It is also true that overall economic conditions as well as individual characteristics have an effect on levels of success, as do gender and race, choice of field of study, and the kind of higher education institution one attends. Still the fact is that going to college and beyond has been and remains a smart choice for most Americans, and they appear to have known that since the end of World War II. The expectation of a brighter future and the fear that without education one was substantially less likely to participate in the American dream turned out to be accurate enough to become self-reinforcing to build and maintain the higher education industry.

Public money helped in producing the growth. Indeed it was probably crucial to the industry. As World War II ended, elite universities worried that expanding higher education through public funding would open the doors to too many unqualified students, thereby cheapening the product. Yet they too soon found themselves caught up in the opportunities of expansion. The Cold War, which made advanced education a weapon against the Soviet threat, combined with an enhanced ideology of equality of opportunity, which took form in an emergent civil rights movement, to propel public investment further. The high stature of research led to investments unparalleled in American history. State pride led to increased investments in state systems of public higher education, while local pride—and the economic gains of large numbers of students and job opportunities—led to demands to have "our" college or university. Federal and state governments reinforced the cycle, either by providing grants to colleges and universities to be redistributed primarily as student aid or by giving funds directly to students, thereby keeping the costs of attending college low and allowing colleges to increase their tuition fees, a situation in which everyone seemed to win.

Perhaps no series of events encapsulated the postwar faith in education than the reaction to the Soviet Union's sending of the Sputnik rocket into space in October 1957 and the subsequent passage of the National Defense Education Act of 1958. What began as a technological and national defense crisis—the Soviets are going to overwhelm the U.S.—quickly became translated into an educational crisis. The immediate response was that American education was at fault and colleges in particular had failed. These harsh attacks that America's students were neither learning enough—too busy doing other things—nor learning the right things (too little science, mathematics, and foreign languages) quickly became converted into the first substantial all-purpose federal legislation and financial support for higher education. As Barbara Barksdale Clowse writes: "The Sputnik crisis transformed the politics of federal aid to education; it altered the terms of the debate and temporarily neutralized much of the opposition. The Cold War rivalry seemed to dictate that the nation mobilize her brain power, including schoolchildren and undergraduate and graduate students, on an emergency basis" (Clowse, 1981, p. 4; Divine, 1993).

Sputnik's launch, followed by a second orbit a month later, shocked the nation. If there was one seemingly immutable assumption that had come out of World War II, it was that the United States was scientifically and technologically ahead of the Soviet Union. That faith was tested when the U.S.S.R. exploded its first atom bomb, but even if the U.S. was no longer the only scientific superpower, it was still nonetheless the most advanced. With the Soviets first into space, nothing seemed secure anymore. Higher education quickly jumped into action, converting a wave of criticism about its failures into calls for federal financial support. Success was almost instantaneous. Three weeks after the launch, the *New York Times* ran the headline, "Eggheads Called Hope of Country" (Oct. 26, 1957, p. 6). Less than a year later, the Congress passed with presidential approval the National Defense Education Act, which authorized $635 million, more than 55 percent of which went to colleges and universities to aid students in the form of loans and graduate fellowships.

Much the same phenomenon occurred in the mid-1960s, when the War on Poverty replaced the Cold War as the basis for federal action in education. The Higher Education Act of 1965 brought together and expanded existing financial aid programs—work/study, student grants and loans, college facilities funds—and joined them to a new focus on access through grants to the financially needy. The Act provided guaranteed student loans for moderate income families and established Upward Bound to improve access for the poor and minorities. Seven years later, the Higher Education Amendments of 1972 went even further, making equality of opportunity the core of federal higher education policy.

The effect of the federal legislation of the late 1950s through the early 1970s, as well as parallel efforts at the state and local levels, was to increase dramatically the stature of higher education, to fund its expansion, and to contain the costs to individuals seeking to go to college and graduate schools. Students and their families responded. College going was truly a field of dreams, providing opportunities for young people to do better than their parents. In absolute terms, between 1950 and 1970 income returns to college graduates increased in a steady fashion. Each annual cohort of college graduates was likely to earn more money than the previous cohorts, as employers heavily recruited college graduates. Relative to high school graduates and high school dropouts, returns to college graduates during those twenty years grew or remained stable annually, again peaking around 1970. In the words of one commentator, "jobs sought graduates" (Gumport, 1997; Hecker, 1992).

There was, it seemed, in the twenty-five years after World War II, little restraint on the possibilities for higher education. Although the 1960s student rebellions provoked substantial criticism, the decade ended with the largest growth higher education had ever seen. Substantial state and federal funding existed; the commitment to civil rights and educational opportunity opened doors for minorities; women were a growing proportion of the college population. Income returns to college graduates were high and had been growing in a seeming unending progression, and the wage gap between women and men and between African-Americans and whites was closing, larger as a result of increased educational opportunities. There was little reason to think that the discontents then surfacing would become any more than discontents, and little reason to believe that the field of dreams was about to be unsettled.

1.3 A field unsettled

The meteoric growth of higher education in the decades after World War II created a large and self-confident industry, one that regularly assured itself that it simultaneously met the public's desires—by strengthening the nation through its research and training of professionals with the capacity to meet the nation's economic and social needs—and the more personal goals of economic returns and professional status to individuals. The criticisms that periodically appeared served primarily to strengthen higher education's commitments to its own successes. Few in higher education expected that the undertones of anger during the 1960s would turn into persistent and threatening discontents during the 1970s and 1980s. As early as 1971, some commentators worried that higher education had lost its capacity to manage itself and suggested that a number of colleges and universities were in serious fiscal trouble. Some critics complained about the continuing lack of access for minorities despite substantial gains, the neglect of undergraduate teaching, the uniformity across institutions, the remoteness of higher education from the rest of society, and its exceedingly close association both with government and with left-leaning social activists. The contradictions among the various criticisms were easily apparent, yet the critics' voices coalesced in the public's mind around the notion that there was something terribly wrong with higher education (Freeland, 1990, pp. 97–115).

Initially, the sourest notes focused on the behavior of students. The protests in the 1960s and early 1970s, the in-your-face dress and provocative language, and the violence of some of the protests raised questions about whether the entitled were worth the expenditure. As a young assistant professor, I encountered President Nixon's urban and domestic affairs advisor, Daniel Patrick Moynihan, soon to become a U.S. Senator, who was also a former advisor of mine. Moynihan was furious and he spoke for many Americans when he angrily complained to me that "even the mathematics students were protesting" and in the wake of the demonstrations and violence at Columbia University, he was apoplectic that parents were bailing their children out of jail and protesting against undue violence on the part of the police. Why didn't these parents, he fumed, let their children take responsibility for their illegal and uncivil actions?

But there was also a deeper malaise affecting higher education after 1970, one that would have an even more substantial impact: the intersection of rising costs of college and stagnant incomes. Higher education presumed that its importance allowed it to increase its expenditures substantially faster than the gross national product, the rate of inflation, and average family annual income. That thinking quickly became an albatross. As the U. S. economy in the 1970s and 1980s faced soaring inflation, high unemployment, oil crises, wage and price controls, loss of markets to Japanese and German goods, and corporate downsizing, the seemingly unconstrained costs of higher education began to look obscene, with tuition increases sometimes going above 10 percent per year.

Concern about costs coincided with uncertainties about the income returns to higher education. After 1970, depending upon the source, income returns to college graduates either flattened, declined, or increased only modestly over the next two decades (Goldin and Katz, 2008; Levy and Murnane, 1992).[1] Although the data were in fact complicated, consensus quickly emerged that going to college was no longer "paying off" in the ways that it had over the previous decades. Why this happened is the source of controversy, with interpretations pointing to an oversupply of college graduates, the deskilling of many managerial and technical jobs, corporate downsizing, the poor quality of elementary and secondary schools, declines in the quality of academic and technical skills possessed by college graduates, lowered admissions standards to college, the larger proportion of female college graduates entering the labor market who were paid on average less than equally schooled males, and a mismatch between the skills college graduates possessed and those required in the advanced labor market.

If the field of dreams got rocky in the 1970s and 1980s, it also became even more imperative to play the game. Relative to high school graduates, the differential earnings to college graduates declined during the 1970s. In 1971, male college graduates aged 25–34 earned 22 percent more, on average, than male high school graduates of the same age. In 1979, the earnings differential had shrunk to 13 percent, thus suggesting that for males it seemed less important to graduate college. For women aged 25–34, the changes were similar, with the earnings premium associated with college education declining from 41 percent in 1971 to 23 percent in 1979

---

[1] The measurement of earnings return is one of the most technically complex areas in the economics of higher education, in part because overall data frequently mask differences by gender, race, and field of study, and because it is extremely difficult to connect income return issues to the state of the economy at any given time. For a summary of studies on returns to college prior to 1990, see Pascarella and Terenzini (1991).

(Levy and Murnane, 1992, pp. 1354–1357). It was thus reasonable to have doubts about going to college in the 1970s, although for women especially the benefits continued to be better than for men.

During the 1980s, in broad terms, graduating from college became an even wiser idea. The educational premium for male college graduates aged 24–35 over the same aged high school graduates jumped from 13 percent in 1979 to 38 percent in 1987; for women in the same categories, the premium rose from 23 percent to 45 percent, but with a substantial difference. Whereas the median real earnings of male high school graduates working full-time declined by 12 percent in the 1980s—as did the likelihood of even working full-time—it did not decline for female high school graduates working full-time (Levy and Murnane, 1992, pp. 1356–1357). In the case of both women and men, the gap between high school and college earnings was even greater, since the likelihood of high school graduates holding full-time jobs year-round declined considerably during the 1980s. With women entering new professions and with the income inequality gap between men and women narrowing, the experiences of college-going for the two sexes had shifted. For men, graduating from college after 1970 was considerably less positive than the golden era between 1945 and 1970; for women, college graduation had become in terms of earnings much more positive. For both, however, the gap between going to college or not going was huge. It quite simply paid to graduate college. This phenomenon has continued into the present and, in fact, has probably increased. The difference between college graduation and high school graduation is substantial (Goldin and Katz, 2008).

If college and beyond has remained enormously important in economic terms, why then did the value of a college education become such a source of controversy? As I suggested earlier, the data on returns to education are often misleading, in that they fail to account for the enormous differences even among groups that went to college. The data are misleading in often not paying enough attention to the impact of fields of study on income returns. The data are often misleading in not emphasizing the impact of cyclical job demands in the labor market. And the data are often misleading in not emphasizing the change in psychology that came to dominate college attendance in the 1980s. College was as much about avoiding falling behind as about optimistically choosing one's future. What one could be reasonably assured of is that your income and occupational prospects were much better if you graduated college than if you simply entered the labor market after high school.

Still, there always existed a kind of shadow around the dramatic growth in higher education and the enthusiasm with which millions of individuals went to college. Academic scholars and the popular press played into a curious debate about whether individuals should go to college, even as few would advise their children not to go. They kept asking the question: did it pay for individuals to go to college rather than enter the workforce directly out of high school? The question had been around for some time. Just after the publication of the report of the President's Commission on Higher Education in 1947, calling for a dramatic expansion of higher education, a Columbia University economist warned against the potential unemployment and underemployment of too many college graduates in an economy that was not producing college-skilled jobs fast enough. Others complained that parents were pushing their resistant children into college. At the height of the Vietnam War, Yale University President Kingman Brewster worried about "involuntary students," those males in college solely to avoid military service. The media's doubts and occasional questioning, however, were at odds with public opinion. A 1965 national survey of public attitudes toward higher education found that when asked how they would advise a young man or young woman who could finance only two years of college but who had a good job offer, 90 percent of the respondents recommended that the young man pass up the job and pursue college and 77 percent said they would give the same advice to a young woman. "Our responses," the survey's authors concluded, "correspond to the findings of earlier research—that Americans think of higher education in terms of income. Newspaper stories and magazine articles from time to time remind the public that every year of education adds so many dollars to income, and it is easy to see that the college graduate has an advantage in the job market" (Survey Research Center, 1965).

The doubts persisted. In 1975 Caroline Bird's *The Case Against College* (1975) argued that college had become a "holding pen" for high school graduates who could not find jobs other than unskilled and poorly-paid ones. Having established that many young people did not want to be there, she concluded that it was not worth the cost for many of the students and their parents, especially for those youth who were likely to wind up at the economically lowest quartile of college graduates. A year later Richard Freeman's *The Overeducated American* (1976) concluded that the United States had become "a society in which the economic rewards to college education are markedly lower than has historically been the case" and that further investments in higher education are likely to earn decreasing rates of return (Freeman, 1976, pp. 4–5). Because there was now an oversupply of college educated people, jobs no longer sought college graduates. That Freeman's overall conclusion was limited to white males got lost in the hyperbole. His own evidence suggested that relative to white males, the returns to higher education would increase for African-Americans and for women. Lost in the resulting discussion was more than half the American population (Levin, 1977).

The media pounded away, using provocative headlines and lead-ins, like "Is College Worth It?" Almost always, however, they reached the same conclusion. The answer to such questions was Yes! (*Newsweek*, April 29, 1985, pp. 66–68). The media raised doubts about the worth of a degree and complained about rising costs, but agreed, as the 1985 *Newsweek* article put it, that "it would be a mistake for any student—or for the nation—to begin believing that the whole enterprise is a waste, that less schooling is better for anyone's child." Commentators argued that going to college was not as profitable as it once was and that it was socially irrational to have so many people attending college, but they rarely, if ever, recommended that young people not go.

The argument over whether it paid to go to college or, more accurately, whether it paid as much as it used to, quickly became tied to a criticism about learning: college students were graduating without knowing very much. To those who reached this conclusion, almost anything could serve as evidence: open enrollment (a place for everyone) and affirmative action which allowed too many unqualified students to enter college, employer complaints that the quality of employee skills was responsible for the economy's troubles, grade inflation and the takeover of higher education by political correctness, declining SAT scores, and the failures of elementary and secondary school education. What was relevant in the public and political realms was that doubts about the worth of degrees coincided with doubts about whether anyone was learning anything anywhere.

The attacks on higher education's economic worth hit like a bombshell during the 1970s and 1980s. The most popular manifestations were stories of Ph.D.s driving taxicabs in major American cities, as the media probed such questions as "Who needs college?" the title of a 1976 *Newsweek* article that pictured a University of Colorado Phi Beta Kappa student working as a day manager in a restaurant (*Newsweek*, April 26, 1976, pp. 60–69). Yet there was something surreal about the controversies over income returns to higher education. Although the hand-wringing was persistent and the criticism intense, economists and the media agreed that there were still substantial economic advantages to graduating from college with a baccalaureate degree. As Ernest Pascarella and Patrick Terenzini concluded in an extensive review of studies done primarily in the 1970s and 1980s, "The evidence in support of this, based on the simple lifetime earnings differential between college graduates and high school graduates, is dramatic and unequivocal." Indeed, they believed, "the evidence on earnings is consistent with that on occupational status in suggesting that completing the bachelor's degree may be the single most important educational step in the occupational and economic attainment process." There may have been controversy about why this was the case and there certainly were differences in returns by ethnicity, gender, class, college or university attended, majors, economic conditions, and individual characteristics, but the bottom line remained the same: it was better to go than not go (Pascarella and Terenzini, 1991, Ch. 11; Grubb, 1992).

The evidence suggests that students and their families agreed that college was, if not a good thing, necessary to get ahead. The percentage of recent high school graduates enrolled in college, which had climbed from 45 percent in 1960 to a height of 55.4 percent in 1968, slid down during the 1970s, but then began to rise again in the 1980s. While there was a brief drop in full time undergraduate enrollments in the early 1970s—partly as a result of the elimination of the draft deferment for college students—and again around 1977 and between 1983 and 1985, the trajectory was upward, sharply between 1973 and 1975, then more gradually between 1977 and 1983, and again after 1985. The number of part-time undergraduates showed a slightly different profile, but the overall trend between 1971 and 1991 was decidedly upward. Among African-Americans, participation rates increased in the 1960s, declined in the early 1970s, increased briefly and then flattened or declined until the mid-1980s, before turning upward again. Among African-Americans, sharp differences by gender appeared with female enrollment increasing between 1976–1985, while male rates went down. Between 1986 and 1990, when participation rates went up for both sexes, they did so by almost 16 percent among African-American women and by about 9 percent for African-American men. Between 1976 and 1990, participation rates for Hispanics and Asian-Americans also increased, with female enrollment in each group increasing more rapidly than male enrollment (Hauptman & McLaughlin, 1992, pp. 168–178).

Despite the unsettling in the field of dreams, higher education seemed to flourish. In the 1980s college costs outpaced inflation while median family income stagnated. Yet enrollments grew from 12.1 million in 1980 to 12.8 million in 1987 (Breneman, 1994, pp. 31–32). For all the expressions of concern about costs and income returns and the doubts about whether it was worth it, tuition at private colleges skyrocketed and grew substantially at public institutions. Endowments flourished as the stock market went upward (broken only by the extreme but short-term crash of 1987). And most surprisingly, federal and state funding kept on growing. Despite the avowed intent of the Reagan administration to reduce federal commitments, federal funding of higher education increased in real dollars between 1980 and 1990 by 42 percent, while state and local funding increased in real dollars by 27 percent (Hauptman, 1992; Hauptman and McLaughlin, 1992).[2]

---

[2] Increased financial aid and tuition discounting helped the flow of students continue. The prevailing wisdom is that financial aid and net tuition costs influence low-income families more than middle- and upper-income families. Direct grants have some impact on whether low-income students go to college, whereas for middle- and upper-income students

Much of this came as a surprise for, as David Breneman (1994) pointed out, the 1980s began on a dreary note. The 1970s had witnessed substantial concerns over higher education's ability to balance its budget, public debate over quality and political correctness, and, as has been discussed, questions about the "over-educated American." The 1980s continued these themes, but began by suggesting that demography was the next great threat to the higher education industry: an anticipated 25 percent decline in the number of 18-year-olds over the next 15 years. Even if larger proportions of high school graduates enrolled in college, the likelihood of actual enrollments dropping by 5 percent to 15 percent was substantial. Combined with high inflation, unemployment, little if any productivity gains, and anticipated drops in real income, the situation looked bleak.

The catastrophic projections at the beginning of the 1980s did not come true, but enough things happened during the decade to shake higher education's foundations. For one, higher education was saved by a dramatic influx of older, nontraditional students, many of them attending part-time. Although their participation had been growing since the 1960s, between 1970 and 1975 the number of students aged 22 or older increased by more than 50 percent, while the number of traditionally-aged students remained relatively constant. Between 1978 and 1989, the number of college students aged 25 and older grew by 44 percent, while the number of 18–24 year-olds in college increased by only 7 percent. The number of female college students in that same period grew by 26 percent, accounting for the largest growth among older students. After 1975, students aged 22 or older became the majority of the college-going population; in the late 1980s, those 30 and older were the fastest growing percentage of matriculates (Gumport, 1997). Older students were also much more likely to enroll part-time in the 1980s, accounting for almost all the growth in part-time attendance. In their determination to enroll in college, older students affirmed

---

such grants influence their choice among colleges rather than whether to go to college at all. The shift from grant aid to loans in the 1980s and 1990s appears to have adversely affected the enrollment of low-income students and constrained their choices since they are less inclined to incur substantial debt. See Hauptman and McLaughlin (1992, pp. 159–185).

what was higher education's greatest triumph: college was the necessary license for middle class status, and they were starting to demand that higher education pay attention to them.

For women, any doubts about the worth of college seemed to get blown away. Women went from 40 percent of the student population to a majority during the 1970s, and up to 54 percent by 1990, and then to 56 percent early in the 21st century. The income returns to women college graduates went up faster than those for men, so that by the end of the 1980s, while women with comparable education and jobs still earned less than men, the wage inequality gap was closing. Women had achieved a comparably greater earnings premium than men for going to college.

The expansion of college-going rates has not been matched by a parallel expansion in degree attainment, and therein lies one of the most unsettling features in the field of dreams. Whereas rates of enrollment among 20–24 year olds increased from 44 percent in 1980 to 61 in 2003, college completion rates did not keep pace. (High school graduation rates similarly slowed down during the period.) As Robert Zemsky pointed out, between 1950 and 1982, "the proportion of those who started, but did not complete, a college education declined from more than half to less than 30 percent. By the 1990s, however, the gap was again widening, as more than 40 percent of those students who started college quit before receiving a baccalaureate degree" (Zemsky, 1997; Gumport, 1997). Goldin and Katz (2008, p. 326) summarize the overall trends as follows: "College-going rates among 20–24 year olds... have increased substantially in the United States—from 44 percent in 1980 to 61 percent in 2003 largely in response to the post-1980 rise in the college wage premium. But college *completion* rates have not kept pace and the United States has fallen to the middle-of-the-pack among OECD nations in four-year college completion rates for recent cohorts." The theme has been reiterated by McPherson, Bowen, and Chingos (2009). Americans became convinced that it was necessary to go to college, but they stopped receiving the degrees that were so much a part of the reason they bothered to attend.

Part of this has to do with a terrible "price-income squeeze" that became serious after 1980 and has continued to undermine higher education's ability to fulfill its aspirations. The direct costs of going to college—tuition, fees, room and board—increased dramatically beginning in the 1980s, initially at private universities and then with an even harsher reality in the public universities, substantially outpacing inflation and the family incomes of most Americans. At the same time median income in constant dollars stayed either the same, declined, or increased only slightly. With financial aid shifting from grants to loans and declines in the proportion of public dollars supporting higher education, the pace of inequality increased. The differences in college attendance rates, Goldin and Katz (2008, p. 149) conclude, "by parental income, race, and ethnicity are large even among students with similar academic grades and achievement test scores. The combination of the high costs of college, credit market constraints, and student debt aversion leaves many youth from poorer and middle-income families behind in the pursuit of a college education."

This has been tragic for the field of dreams retains its extraordinarily powerful pull. High school graduates are still seeking to attend college in substantial numbers. New populations are attending in record-breaking numbers, signifying how powerful higher education's license to middle class income, respectability and status has become. For the selective colleges and universities that promise entry into the upper class, the fight to get in has all the characteristics of a gold rush. Income returns to college as compared to high school continue to be high. As David Breneman (1994, pp. 31–32) wrote, "Largely because the bottom fell out of the job market for high school graduates [especially for males], the economic returns to a college education reversed itself, with the wage premium for college graduates increasing between 1979 and 1986 to larger than those found in any earlier period" (Breneman, 1994, pp. 31–32). Goldin and Katz (2008) and McPherson, Bowen, and Chingos (2009) make clear that income returns to higher education remain high today.

The rush for gold through college access continues, but the institution of higher education seems shaky, more uncertain today than at any time in the last 60 years. A huge proportion of those who believe it is necessary to go to college to succeed are finding it hard to attain a degree. Those who hope that higher education will translate into high incomes are finding just paying for college harder and harder and, when they get out, must worry about finding or holding a job and paying their debts. And without a college education, one would be in even bigger fiscal trouble. During the last decade a hard and perhaps embittering reality has set in. Going to and graduating from college is a near necessity for those who aspire to get ahead, it is a necessary route to professions that are unavailable without a degree or increasingly without more than one degree. With the labor market for high school graduates in a continuing state of disrepair, college and beyond really is necessary. But even those who recognize it are stumbling badly. The field of dreams has become a troubled place.

CHAPTER 2

Higher education as vocational education[*]

Will this help me get a better job?
(Frequently Asked Question)

For students and their families, it is the most important question. It is also, within limits and with lots of caveats, an answerable question. In terms of should one stay in school, go to college, get a first diploma, and consider continuing on for a post-first degree program, the answer is yes. More definitive answers require all sorts of caveats. Good economic times help, as do cycles of enthusiasm for certain kinds of training and shortages in selected occupations. Graduating with a bachelor's degree helps. Certain majors help more than others. For professions that require post-baccalaureate degrees, continuing on after college is a necessity. The reputation of the college or university one attends helps. Grades help a little, though their importance is usually mediated through their utility in getting one into higher status institutions or programs. And, of course, personal characteristics also play a role, as do race and gender. So if the question about getting a better job matters, then there are lots of things to consider beyond staying in school. The answer may be yes, but it is not that simple.

2.1 The education gospel and vocationalism

One of the most extraordinary developments of the last century has been the worldwide growth in educational opportunity. For most of the 20th century the United States led the way, but in the last decades many other countries have been increasing educational opportunities at a bewildering pace; Canada, China, and Russia are examples, but the trend is worldwide (Altbach, Reisberg, and Rumbly, 2009).

---

[*] Earlier versions of this chapter were co-authored with W. Norton Grubb.

The growing importance now attributed to education is to be valued, and in the criticisms presented in this chapter, I do not mean to diminish education's positive contributions to social and economic goals and to the expansion of opportunities for millions of people. But education's promises are often exaggerated and its aspirations thwarted, and these too are important to understand.

Every country has its own story about the role of education. In what W. Norton Grubb and I call the Education Gospel (Grubb and Lazerson, 2004), the United States version of this story promotes an emphasis on formal schooling for its economic contributions— to the society and to the individual. The story is essentially accurate (Goldin and Katz, 2008), but it has so many different parts, that blindly believing in it can be misleading. In broad outlines, the Education Gospel is based on a particular vision of the present and the future that goes something like this: The Knowledge Revolution (or the Information Society, or the communications revolution) has dramatically changed and continues to change the nature of economic development and work, shifting emphasis away from occupations once rooted in industrial production to occupations associated with knowledge, information, and technology. This transformation has both increased the skills required for new occupations and updated the three R's, enhancing the importance of what are often referred to as "higher-order" skills including communications skills, problem-solving, and advanced reasoning. Obtaining these skills increasingly requires formal schooling past the high school level, so that college (especially completing a degree) is necessary for the jobs of the future. This vision fuels the emphasis in the United States and elsewhere on increased levels of schooling, now apparent world-wide, as well as increasing demands by individuals that they be supported in their efforts to obtain college and university degrees. Around the world the view that getting a post-high school degree (or its equivalent outside the U.S.) has become gospel, something that more and more people believe makes "common sense."

This "common sense" wisdom extends to the kinds of skills needed for economic success, for the Education Gospel maintains that individuals are more likely to find their skills are becoming obsolete because of the pace of technological change. To keep up with advances in technology, individuals need new kinds of skills, especially the capacity to continue to learn and to solve problems, as well as needing personal skills (sometimes called "soft" skills) like independence, initiative, and to be able to work in teams. Because these needs evolve over time, lifelong learning has emerged as one of the significant bell-weathers of the Education Gospel, opening up opportunities for traditional educational institutions and new (and rapidly developing) lifelong learning agencies that offer internet based education. New forms of work organization—especially contingent and part-time labor, with employers hiring temporary rather than permanent workers in order to increase the flexibility of hiring as technologies, products, and economic pressures change— have exacerbated job-changing, further reinforcing the need for lifelong learning. Workers and managers need to have a greater variety of skills, since they are likely to have multiple tasks and multiple jobs in their lifetimes. Economic globalization has meant that no developed country wants to become 'underdeveloped' by relying on raw materials and unskilled labor, further pushing public policies to expand educational opportunities over one's lifespan. For developing countries the goal is to use a combination of education and technology to increase economic progress. The Education Gospel with its call for ever expanding education systems thus provides the basis for meeting the economic challenges of the present and future—with worldwide consequences.

The Education Gospel resonates with individuals by providing them with a powerful rationale and incentives to use education to 'get ahead'. It states clearly that success depends upon the power of higher education to provide them with skills to facilitate entry into the labor market for professionals. The Gospel's rhetorical power comes from its ability to unify individual aspirations of success and national goals of economic development, or in the case of the higher education efforts of the European Union, to create a powerful European-wide economy (Matei, 2008). Nations have a rationale for expanding their higher education systems and individuals have a rationale for staying in school. In both the national version and the individual version, the purpose of higher education becomes primarily and overwhelmingly economic.

The connection between the Education Gospel, economic development, and vocational preparation is a global phenomenon. The

European Union has made the knowledge economy the centerpiece of its higher education efforts (Matei, 2008; van Vught, 2009). Great Britain has been searching for "key" or "core" skills for decades; Germany has an extensive list of key qualifications for work in the knowledge society and is seeking to develop its universities to contribute more directly to economic growth. Australia has been worrying about its higher education system failing to keep up with economic globalization for decades. Emerging economies in Eastern Europe and in Asia (including China) are following their own forms of the Education Gospel to justify expanding education. All over the globe, countries have discovered the importance of the Knowledge Revolution requiring higher levels of education and technologically-based forms of human capital as ways of competing economically (Altbach, Reisberg, and Rumbley, 2009).

None of this is entirely new, since education has always been tied to economic goals. Before the 20th century, however, ideas about education's contribution to economic development and individual success were usually described in terms of higher education's contributions to public service and to the preparation of knowledgeable individuals with high moral character. In the course of the 20th century, accelerating during the last half of the century, the economic purposes of higher education became embedded in a set of vocational educational practices within educational institutions whose primary purpose became preparation for occupational roles. Vocationalism is an awkward but useful term referring not primarily to traditional vocational education but to preparation for *vocations*—occupations as careers or professions rather than mere jobs, employment that provides personal meaning, economic benefits, continued development over one's life, social status and connections to the greater society. Germans use the word *Beruf* to refer to one's profession and, along with it, to the implied belief that one must develop multiple capacities for successful professional practice. Professional education is the term most often applied to this vocational orientation in higher education.

In the United States a vocationalized system of education emerged in fits and starts, beginning with changes in high schools and the establishment of university-based professional schools at the end of the 19th century. It accelerated over the course of the 20th century, referred to by Goldin and Katz (2008) as "the century of human capital." This has been the most substantial transformation in American schooling over the past century, and increasingly in other countries, opening the door to enormous growth in enrollments, as well many other changes in the purposes of education, the curriculum, the meaning of college attendance, the mechanisms of upward mobility, the mechanisms of inequality, conceptions of equity, and the education-based pillar of the American Dream. The vocationalization of education takes different forms, depending upon whether it is located in high schools, four-year colleges and universities, community colleges, technology institutes, job training programs and adult education, although there are enough common features across each level and institution to call it vocationalism.

2.2 The U.S. approach to vocationalism

The most obvious consequence of the Education Gospel has been its role in transforming the purposes of schooling from civic and moral purposes (in grammar schools) or mental discipline and character development for potential leaders (in higher education) to occupational preparation. This process has happened in slightly different ways at different levels of education. Changes in high schools around 1900—the shift from civic to occupational purposes and the creation of different vocational tracks—were particularly influential in leading to the view that formal schooling is important for economic purposes. These changes were most obviously responses to the decline of apprenticeships as a basic form of work preparation, as well as ways to keep teenage boys in school beyond age 14. Vocationally-oriented schooling had lots of advantages over apprenticeships, since it concentrated on learning rather than simply doing routine work and it opened up opportunities to enter occupations traditionally closed to women and minorities. These advantages have continued into the present. While practice-based preparation for occupations and professions provides hands-on, real-life experiences, which are often quite advantageous, workplace-based learning, like internships, are often reduced to low-skilled repetitive practices, like copying materials, typing on a computer, or making coffee, without a lot of attention paid to progressive development of skills and understanding. Individuals participating in such hands-on learning programs too often become inexpensive part-time low-skilled labor. Formal schooling does not necessarily prepare skilled workers and professionals much better, but it does have the possibility of extending young people's literacy and numeric skills in ways that improve their opportunities to achieve professional status.[1]

The transformation of higher education in the U.S. has been inextricably linked to the emergence of the modern professions. The process of emphasizing vocationally-based higher education proceeded in fits and starts, starting with the Morrill Act of 1862 "to promote the liberal and practical education of the industrial classes in the several pursuits and professions in life," continuing with the development of professional schools in the last half of the 19th century, and greatly expanding in urban centers and then in the massive expansion of higher education after 1960. The process led to differentiated institutions of higher education. Elite research universities, for example, emphasize research and post-baccalaureate education while incorporating older forms of liberal education at the undergraduate level. Regional universities, which developed from schools of education and agriculture, are much less selective and concentrate on overtly professional majors in business, health professions, engineering and communications, as well as numerous other smaller fields of study. Traditional liberal arts colleges tend to divide into one of two groups. The minority group continues to emphasize the liberal arts, anticipating that large numbers of the graduates will go on to masters and doctoral programs, all of which are vocational by definition, since they overtly prepare people for jobs. The majority of liberal arts colleges add more and more professional majors to their curriculum and diminish considerably their allegiance to the traditional liberal arts. Even some traditional academic majors, like economics and psychology, which would seem not to be explicitly vocational, are in practice oriented toward occupational preparation. The fact is that two-thirds to three-quarters of undergraduates are majoring in fields with overtly vocational goals,

---

[1] Grubb and Lazerson (2004, ch. 7) develop these issues and describe ways that school-based and work-based education programs can be integrated to capture the benefits of both.

and the proportions are much higher in regional universities (Brint et al. 2002).

Community colleges represent the most dramatic manifestation of the shift to vocational goals. From their early emphasis on academic education and the transfer of students into bachelor degree colleges and universities, community colleges became increasingly dedicated to occupational preparation, particularly in response to a persistent mid-20th century version of the Education Gospel that argued that the U.S. would have increasing need for more technical workers and semi-professionals. By the 1980s these views had positioned the community college as preeminently vocationally oriented, ready to add a multiplicity of occupational programs including upgraded training for incumbent workers, retraining for workers who need to shift occupations, and remedial training for welfare recipients and the long-term unemployed, while still retaining academic education. (Grubb, 1996).

Less noticed in all of this is that vocationalism has been the driving force of higher education's expansion. Indeed it is hard to imagine a mass higher education system that was not focused on occupational preparation. Every level of schooling in the United States above elementary school has expanded by becoming vocationalized. The high school expanded in the 1920s and 1930s, universities expanded in the 1920s and then the 1960s, community colleges boomed after 1960. The segments of education dedicated to purely intellectual or moral traditions—elite liberal-arts colleges, a few private religious colleges, a few selective public high schools and some private high schools dedicated to older academic traditions—have dwindled in relative importance.

In the American approach to education, expansion has taken place in comprehensive educational institutions. While there remain a few specialized high schools in large cities, a few technical institutes, and some specialized post-secondary institutions in music, the arts, and in psychology, overall, educational institutions in the U.S. have been comprehensive, that is, institutions that offer a wide variety of courses and programs. The American preference for comprehensive institutions partly reflects equity goals, of giving all students an equal chance to succeed at what they choose, rather than have students channeled into specialized schools. More important-

ly, students have also voted with their feet, preferring comprehensive institutions that maximize choice and keep the promise of further education open. Vocational institutions themselves tend to want to
become comprehensive as a way of adding status through academic
programs and through being able to advertise that their students can
choose either to enter labor markets directly or to continue on with
advanced education. This has been most apparent in the shift of historically teacher training and agricultural colleges into comprehensive universities in the 1960s and 1970s and the recent trend of two-
year community colleges becoming universities.

All of this has a self-reinforcing affect. As more and more occupations come to require school- or university-based preparation and
as students and parents then lobby for entry into education for economic reasons, the shift away from 'experiential' learning toward
formal schooling accelerates. A particularly vivid example of this
involves the occupational preparation of visual artists, actors,
dancers, musicians, and filmmakers. Traditionally such artists made
their way by developing their skills on their own, working at various jobs, and learning from each other — the Impressionists working in Paris around 1900 or the abstract expressionists, poets, filmmakers, and writers in New York's Greenwich Village during the
1950s. In contrast 'academic training' in formal art schools had a
pejorative connotation, typically viewed as regurgitating old art,
emphasizing classroom copying rather than creating new art forms.
Beginning some time in the 1980s, however, most artists in the U.S.
began to earn a bachelor's or master's degree in fine arts from a
conventional university or art school, a practice increasingly adopted by actors, musicians, dancers, and filmmakers. Such schooling
provides access to complex tools and equipment (computers, video
and audio equipment, kilns), to a community of other artists, to the
credentials necessary for teaching jobs, and to education in the history and theory of art, including ways of thinking that are newly
important in conceptual art. In highly competitive professions, the
art degree opens doors to employment in the art world, including
jobs in museums, galleries, video production, management, and
teaching that do not involve producing art so much as keeping artists
in touch with current developments. The master of fine arts (MFA)
degree has itself become increasingly necessary for teaching jobs

in the arts. Occupations that once epitomized freedom from formal schooling have thus become credentialed, in ways similar to accounting, teaching, and dentistry (Tomkins, 2002).

New occupations have evolved in the same way, striving to develop the status of professions with required levels of education and certification. The occupations based on computers and electronics began with computer programmers whose preparation in the 1960s and 1970s was informal: programmers learned by reading manuals and by doing. Gradually, however, programming moved into formal schooling, with baccalaureate programs for programmers; sub-baccalaureate programs for those working with applications (e.g., word processing and spreadsheet programs); and graduate programs for those aiming to enter research and development. The cycle of informal preparation superseded by formal schooling is now being replicated in internet-related occupations, where at first individuals prepared by learning HTML and website design on their own. Then programs were created in community colleges and subsequently drifted into four-year institutions incorporating elements of design, programming, and marketing, often under the label of multimedia (Villeneuve, 2000). None of these school-based programs are absolutely necessary for entry into these new professions, in the way that they are for the formally licensed professions like law and medicine. But for all of these occupations, formal schooling has become increasingly the dominant path of entry.

The reorganization of work also generates new specialties that become distinct occupations with their own educational requirements, reinforcing the cycle of vocationally-driven schooling. Business has created sub-occupations with specialized programs, including those for purchasing agents, sales representatives, accounting, insurance, and actuarial science, hospitality services management, real estate, and apparel and accessories marketing. Medicine has become increasingly fragmented, leading to the emergence of school-based programs for physicians' assistants, certified nurse practitioners and nurse's aides, midwife-practitioners, cardiac technologists, radiological technicians, and physical therapists. Law has spawned paralegals and legal secretaries; engineers have begotten engineering technicians; architects have sired architectural drafting; and accountants now rely on para-accountants and spreadsheet specialists trained in community colleges. Of course, talented individuals can still find their way into many of these occupations without formal credentials in ways they cannot to become medical doctors and lawyers. But in all these occupations formal schooling is increasingly the way to go.

Educational institutions themselves contribute to the pressures for vocationalism, particularly by engaging in competition for additional students. The most typical form of institutional competition is to open new programs as demand develops. Almost every suggestion for a new program comes with an assessment of the anticipated job market, and state agencies typically ask for data on the demand for the program before approving it in public universities. In addition, education institutions strive for higher status through "institutional drift"—by offering degrees for jobs higher in the occupational hierarchy. Most public comprehensive universities used to be normal schools preparing teachers; many of them subsequently became comprehensive state colleges serving undergraduates with a few master's level programs. Some of these, as has happened in California, make the claim that they should be allowed to offer the Ph.D., the mark of a true research university. At the sub-baccalaureate level, regional vocational schools, established in the 1970s to provide vocational education to clusters of high schools, adopted adult vocational programs and then became technical institutes. Technical institutes become comprehensive community colleges. The pressure from community colleges now is to provide baccalaureate degrees as add-ons to their associate degree programs. This kind of institutional drift contributes to more and more institutions providing occupational credentials at higher levels.

Reinforcement has also come from students seeking to amplify their professional qualifications. Once vocationalism is underway, more schooling becomes necessary for students as a form of self-defense, particularly if they want access to the highest status and best paying professions. The students need only look at the competition in front of them: entry into high-status professional schools and four-year colleges is fierce. Battles over access, the use of standardized entrance tests, and affirmative action result in political and legal wars. And the escalation of credentials seems to have no end. Increasingly undergraduates are earning credits in two, three, and sometimes even four majors as a way of gaining an advantage in the job market. Graduate students in engineering, law, medicine, and business are enrolling in multiple or combined programs like Biotechnolgy and Business or Law and Medicine. Given the dominant equation that more schooling leads to better jobs, there seems little likelihood of the tide turning.

Amid all of this, the liberal arts whithered. They did not die, but they are certainly not flourishing. Mostly, what used to be thought of as the liberal arts are dead-ended in general education courses offered, where they exist, primarily during the first year of college, with occasional snatches in the second year. They are the appetizers before the main dish, the major or in many instances today, the majors that lead to the labor market and the professions, sometimes directly, or sometimes through enrollment in post-first degree professional schools. It is possible to think about a reinvigorated argument for liberal arts education, but this requires giving them a purpose beyond the vague conception that introductions to literature, languages, history, and the natural sciences are necessary if one is to be considered educated. To achieve a firmer and more aggressive argument for liberal arts education, however, requires understanding where the notion of liberal arts came from and what has happened to it.

What later became the liberal arts once had clear purposes, goals that were inextricably bound to education. In the early 19th century collegiate education was structured around shaping the mind through certain subject-based exercises and providing the mind with the essential elements of moral character. In more concrete terms this meant studying Latin, Greek, mathematics, philosophy, literature, and other such subjects that trained the mind much like sport activities trained the body, for the mind was thought of as a muscle whose various parts could be strengthened by appropriate mental exercises. The subjects themselves were important because they prepared students for their roles as leading citizens. Knowledge of languages, mathematics, literature, and philosophy was expected to produce educated leaders with the capacity to make wise and good decisions. The package was powerful, but in the context of an increasingly economic-driven society, it was unsustainable (Thelin, 2004).

Professionally oriented courses entered the curriculum in increasing numbers, almost invariably associated with attracting students, providing them with a justification for spending time in school rather than working. By the end of the 19th century, a more clearly articulated notion of preparing young people directly for the labor market had evolved. The liberal arts still retained a hold, less because they trained the mind muscle or signified that one was prepared or should be for public leadership, but more because their continuing value as emblematic of being educated, if not learned. In the decades between the end of World War I and the 1950s, the liberal arts received a substantial boost as part of globalization—although that word was not yet in vogue. Two world wars in less than 30 years, a devastating world-wide economic depression in the 1930s, the horrors of fascism and the looming presence of the Soviet Union, strengthened the belief that exposure to the liberal arts—literature, history, foreign languages, and the sciences—would give students a better sense of their responsibilities as democratic citizens and improve their capacity to act on those responsibilities. This noble idea virtually collapsed after 1960 as the waves of students entered higher education in search of economic rewards and as faculty turned increasingly to disciplines and specializations, leaving both students and faculty in the pleasant position of agreeing that the liberal arts were not all that important.

The result was a rush to make the liberal arts more relevant, almost exclusively through general education requirements. This usually takes one of two forms. The first is to create special interdisciplinary courses in the first year allowing students to choose among them. Almost always the courses are spiced up with attractive titles. Whether students like them or not depends upon the theatrical abilities of the instructors. The second alternative is to designate introductory courses in the existing disciplines as appropriate general education courses, allowing students some leeway in choosing in which discipline they want to be 'generally educated'. Since many instructors view the introductory course in their discipline as an introduction to more advanced courses, there is often not very much general education in them. To some students general education courses look like they are there just to fill in time. There are some ways out of this quandary by, for example, expanding the number and range of interdisciplinary majors so that introductory courses can be broadened, or by taking important and powerful themes like environmental development or finding peace in a world where wars are a constant, and converting them into liberal arts courses. While almost every college and university engages regularly in revising its general education requirements, in fact, there does not seem to be a lot of enthusiasm for the efforts.

It is easy to be discouraged about seeing higher education simply as a transmission belt from learning into economic roles. This is especially the case when extended schooling has many other benefits. It seems to increase levels of tolerance and the capacity to problem solve, for example. Schooling has clearly been central to efforts to increase equity. Educational institutions are more inclusive than a system of job entry based on personal contacts and family connections. When degrees become the primary criterion for jobs, educational inclusiveness opens doors to women, racial minorities, immigrants, gays, and other groups traditionally discriminated against. It is hard to imagine the equity gains of the last half century without a tight connection between formal schooling and labor markets. For better and for worse, the American system of higher education has become dominated by vocational goals and in the process it has produced an enormous increase in education levels and economic opportunities.[2]

2.3 The conflicts of vocationalism

That said, the problems generated by an ever demanding emphasis on vocational outcomes are substantial. The most obvious of these has been a dramatic decline in the civic, moral, and intellectual purposes of education. Public schooling in the United States initially developed with civic and moral goals and the value of education

---

[2] While they correctly point out that different groups have benefited differently from the expansion of educational opportunities, Goldin and Katz (2008) make abundantly clear that staying in school is an advantageous decision. They also make clear that many young people currently are not taking advantage of the schooling available to them and therefore are substantially limiting their occupational and economic opportunities.

for citizenship continues to be frequently reiterated—although it is often so rhetorical that it is usually hard to take seriously. Less frequently there are appeals to disconnect higher education from immediate vocational goals, usually by suggesting that skills connected to reading literature, learning history, and understanding social science methodologies and the natural sciences greatly improve a broad range of analytic abilities, which can then be applied to work situations. Often these appeals are connected to calls for a resuscitated general education in the liberal arts, as well as limitations on the proliferation of professional majors and degrees. Overall, however, the basic message is the same: where students have real choices and are predominantly motivated by occupational goals, there seems to be a relentless diminution of the civic and moral purposes of schooling. The liberal arts have given way to general education, which is usually a smorgasbord of different courses with limited appeal. Students mainly just want to get them over with so they can get on to the real business of education, namely their professionally oriented majors. Instead of serious liberal arts coursework, colleges have substituted communications skills and critical thinking and other such vague notions of education, so that you can teach pretty much anything if you can claim it contributes to the needed skills of the 21st century. In a world where student choice co-exists with professors' reluctance to teach outside their own specializations, it seems that almost anything goes. Attention to civic and moral education is not usually among them.[3]

Less a conflict and more a manifestation of the confusion that surrounds vocational or professional education is the ambiguity of what we mean by vocationalism. One meaning involves *occupational intentions*, when students and others view the purpose of higher education as occupational preparation. This obviously is what professional majors and professional schools are meant to do.

---

[3] Over the last few decades, highly publicized efforts to give civic and moral or ethical education greater place in higher education have appeared. These function best when they are genuinely integrated into the academic basis of the courses. How effective these are in creating a stronger sense of civic and community responsibility remains uncertain. For a fervent call for civic education, see Colby, et al. (2007).

Whether this is actually occurring in a professional program is not always clear, and parents, professors, students, and the institution itself may disagree about whether the intention is being fulfilled. This may lead to conflicts between instructors promoting intellectual engagement and students viewing schooling in purely instrumental terms, i.e., 'Will this really help me get a better job?'

A second meaning of vocationalism depends on whether an institution's subject matter is directed toward overtly vocational ends—the criterion of an *occupational curriculum*. Like occupational intent, this concept at first seems simple: professional programs in universities, community colleges, and technical institutes all have occupational curricula designed to prepare students for particular occupations. But here too, what exactly an occupational curriculum is has been contested. Except in narrowly-defined job training, differences exist over what curriculum produces the most effective workers—over the appropriate skills to teach, the appropriate mix of academic (or theoretical) versus vocational (or applied) coursework, the balance between school-based learning and work-based learning in internships, and the best pedagogy for teaching vocational competencies. Indeed, in most occupational areas debates over the curriculum are among the most heated issues. What kind of curriculum really makes a good doctor, teacher, businessperson, or a good anything else?

A third conception of vocationalism, *related employment,* involves the connection between education and employment. A fully vocationalized education program is one in which the large majority of its graduates find employment in the occupational area for which they have been trained. But when a program's completers enter diverse occupations, as do university students in the humanities, then we tend not to consider the program vocational. In other cases a program can be vocational in *intent* and *curriculum*, but its completers fail to find related employment. Not being able to find employment in the occupation one has presumably been prepared for can be demoralizing, but it rarely has anything to do with the curriculum one has studied. Short- and long-term labor market oversupplies, as well as the reputation of the institution from which one has graduated (assuming one graduates, which is often not the case), play critical roles. Whatever the actual reasons, the failure of related employment produces anger and gives an institution a bad reputation.

This kind of problem is generally avoided with a fourth version of vocationalism—*required schooling*, when a particular kind of schooling is an absolute requirement to enter an occupation: medical school for doctors, Ph.D. programs for professors, and pre-baccalaureate licenses for aviation mechanics, for example. Here too the failure of a credentialed specialist to find work in the specialty may have little to do with the actual program of study, since market conditions and institutional reputations are fairly determinative. The consolation is that the graduate knows that without a required credential, he or she will not even be considered.

When education or training programs fail to satisfy all four of these criteria, conflict is almost inevitable. Some institutions are clearly vocational by all of these criteria, but others are vocational only according to one or two of these attributes. The alignment of all four conceptions of vocationalism is rare precisely because non-vocational components persist; almost all vocational programs try to teach other things than the components of the occupation. The degree to which non-strictly occupational components are included always reflects the level of agreement and disagreement about the purposes of education. But most of all, it turns out to be very hard to actually align educational programs and employment requirements—which also turns out to be the dirty little secret few want to talk about. Even as colleges and universities have become increasingly vocational, conflicts emerge—not only with older, pre-vocational conceptions of schooling, but also among the different strands of a fully vocational form of education.

One of the reasons for this is ironic: the shift of work preparation into education institutions has effectively separated work preparation from work itself. This separation has caused many difficulties in the school-to-work transition, problems that *necessarily* arise once schooling is separated from employment (Ryan, 2001). Schools cannot simply become the same as workplaces. This has led to mechanisms linking schooling and work, ranging from informal to formal. The first encompasses various efforts particularly through career information and guidance (CIG) and through internships to prepare students to be rational choosers. If these mechanisms work well, then students emerge from education knowledgeable about the variety of occupational options and their educational requirements, and capable of making rational (or self-interested) decisions among them. However, when these mechanisms work poorly, as often occurs in high schools and community colleges (National Research Council, 2003) then students are left misinformed, make the wrong decisions, and wind up in occupations for which they are unsuited and in which they are dissatisfied. When this occurs the waste of education and of personal damage to the individual is high.

A different linkage mechanism relies on direct connections between educational institutions and workplaces. Examples include school-business partnerships, advisory committees, customized training in which technical institutes provide training for specific firms, and a co-operative system where schools and employers jointly prepare workers. But here too the quality of these linkages varies greatly. In the U.S. these are largely informal and ineffective. Where these connections are weak, the possibilities for educational preparation becoming disconnected from work requirements increases. The hope is that educational institutions will provide theoretical grounding and analytic skills, while the workplace teaches on-the-job competences and the culture of work. In practice, the connections are usually imprecise and may even be dysfunctional, leading to the common complaint that the student entered the workplace without knowing anything about work.

A third linkage mechanism includes a variety of credentials, licenses, and qualifications, again ranging from highly formalized to informal. When an educational credential works as intended, it provides uniform expectations among all participants. The credential or license informs everyone that the individual is competent. Employers can specify the competencies they need; education and training programs use credential requirements to shape their curriculum and motivate students with the promise of employment; and students know what competencies they must master to become marketable. This is the positive sense of credentials, as market-making devices coordinating the activities of employers, education providers, and students. However, credentials are not really set by the market; they do not just happen because every one understands what is needed. They require considerable institutional effort to create and to enforce, and require three distinct elements: (1) competencies or standards must be established; (2) methods of assessing competencies must be created; and (3) a mechanism for policing the process must be developed. Each of these is complex and potentially controversial, and can be implemented in many different ways ranging from laissez-faire to highly bureaucratic. If any of these three elements are inconsistent with the others, then the value of a credential becomes uncertain and "credentialism" takes on the negative connotation of educational requirements not rationally related to employment requirements. If, for example, employers hire on the basis of experience and ignore degrees and diplomas, then credentials may become superfluous. If the competencies taught are not those required on the job, then both students and employers are disappointed with the results. When jobs require skills (like highly specific skills) that schools cannot or should not teach, then the mismatch generates employer complaints that students lack necessary skills. And, as always, the nature of credentials varies substantially among countries. In the U.S. with its historic tendency toward laissez-faire government, there is very little effort (except for licensed occupations and professions) to codify the content of credentials; most credentials are informal and depend on the reputation of educational institutions, rather than being monitored by an external agency, and so their quality varies enormously.

The mechanisms linking vocationalized education to employment have therefore been the subject of extensive dissatisfaction and debate. The resolution of these debates varies widely, and the positive and negative meanings of credentialism depend on the nature of these solutions. The point here is that once preparation for work has been separated from work itself, such problems are inevitable. Without strong government or industry or professional association intervention, shaping or even determining the competences to be taught for different occupations or jobs within occupations, the connections between schooling and employment are left uncertain.

Vocationalism also remains controversial because of its ambiguous effect on equity. Equality of educational opportunity has been a centerpiece of U.S. educational policy since the Supreme Court's 1954 *Brown v. Board of Education* ruling that state-mandated segregation is unconstitutional. That decision signaled a critical role for schooling at every level, for it argued that education was crucial to economic opportunity. Although originally focused on elementary schools, over the decades the growing vocational importance of higher education intensified struggles around access to and success in colleges and universities, in large measure because the consequences for earnings, class standing, and upward mobility had become so enormous. The expansion of access, particularly to universities, extended education to groups who had previously not had much chance at higher education including more working class students, minority, and immigrants. *Greater* access, however, has not meant *equitable* access. About 25 percent of each college age cohort in the U.S., and even greater percentages of low-income, African-American, and Latino students, still fail to complete secondary education, even as there have been efforts to expand higher education. As higher education has become more important, the failure to complete high school has grown to entail disastrous consequences.

In addition, the "new students" in post-secondary education have gained access to institutions increasingly differentiated along occupational lines: elite universities and elite liberal arts colleges preparing for the highest professions; regional or second-tier universities with lower levels of resources and lower rates of completion, aiming at lower-level semi-professions and managerial jobs; and community colleges with even lower levels of resources and rates of completion, preparing for middle-skilled jobs—implying that greater access does not mean equal access to the same kind of institution, the same levels of resources, or the same kinds of occupational outcomes. And, these inequalities become compounded when the incompletion rates are included. The differentiation of every education institution along roughly occupational lines has been both *horizontal*—in differences among tracks and programs, like the university-bound track in secondary schools distinct from tracks unlikely to lead to university, or engineering majors distinct from education majors—and *vertical* in differences among institutions preparing for different levels of the occupational structure. It is hard to imagine a vocationalized system of education that is not differentiated in this way, as long as doctors and lawyers require different amounts and kinds of schooling than do accountants and teachers, clerks and auto mechanics. This means that the all-too familiar differences of income and class, of race and ethnicity, of foreign birth and language status, and of gender show up in the outcomes, now through the mechanisms of vocationalism and educational attainment rather than through the direct transmission of status via families.

It also appears that vocationalism undermines learning itself, which is counter-intuitive since vocational preparation is supposed to increase student motivation to learn. Unfortunately, evidence is now mounting that when students think of schooling in purely utilitarian and credentialist terms, then they have every reason to get away with as little work as possible as long as they obtain the credentials necessary for employment. Cox (2009) powerfully shows this in her study of students in community colleges, determining that they are highly vocationalist in their orientation, concerned overwhelmingly with schooling as a mechanism of economic advancement and therefore suspicious of anything (including related academic coursework and general education) that appears to be irrelevant. Their most common and important question is, "Why do I have to learn this?" The students tend to view learning as accumulating facts and thus believe that discussions instructors use as a way of exploring different conceptions and attitudes are a waste of time. The students become highly credentialist in the sense that they view the grades and credits they accumulate as the most essential aspect of education, rather than thinking that the grades and credits are representations of their accumulated learning. They consistently make cost-benefit decisions about whether extra effort is worth it. How little do they have to do in order to get an assignment accepted: "What's the least amount of change I need to make to get the paper accepted?" Although Cox's analysis focuses on community college students, the results appear to be readily applicable to a large number of college and university students. The dominant ethos of vocational relevance may in fact be consistently undermining the very learning and the broader competencies that would prepare them best for the long run.

2.4 What's right and what's wrong

It's easy to poke fun at the excesses of the Education Gospel and its rhetoric of renewal through education, but we should understand how much of it is truly admirable. The Gospel places its faith in education for the salvation of a society—rather than, for example, geographic expansion, colonialism, a hyper-active militarism or free-market ideology. Education has in so many places carried the hopes of civilization, and a vision that reinforces its value is surely to be admired. A second positive element is that the Education Gospel has consistently paid attention to the *public* dimensions of schooling, including its potential value in economic growth and in promoting equity and social cohesion, rather than emphasizing individual benefits only. As a result it has justified the public expenditures necessary to expand schooling. Finally, the Education Gospel has expanded the goals of educational institutions, making them richer enterprises where students and teachers alike can establish connections among the political, moral, and economic aspects of society, where the vocational and the academic can be explored simultaneously. The vocational goals of education become objectionable only when they displace all non-vocational purposes. But the worst excesses of the Education Gospel should not blind us to the expansive possibilities of adding new purposes to old institutions.

However, the Education Gospel also contains a number of failings. The most obvious is that it constantly exaggerates the pace of change. The enormous transformations in occupations, from agricultural labor to manufacturing occupations to service work to "knowledge" work, have taken place over two *centuries*. The pace of change today may be faster than in the past, but it is important not to exaggerate, otherwise we risk a kind of 'Chicken Little' scenario in which we are always talking about and acting as if the sky was about to fall in a matter of minutes or an Armageddon scenario with a giant meteorite about to crash. It looks like about 70 percent of new jobs in the near future will require no more than a high school education, and about 75 percent will require no more than modest on-the-job training. Occupational changes will continue to unfold, but the cataclysmic language of the Education Gospel is simply unwarranted.

In developed countries the real problem may in fact not be *under*-education, but a newer problem of *over*-schooling—of levels of schooling that are too high for the occupations individuals are likely to have. Indeed, in several countries including the U.S., England, and Germany the evidence suggests that perhaps 35–40 percent of workers are over-educated for the jobs they hold (Hardtog, 2000). While there may be counter-examples among rapidly-developing countries, in China and India, for example, in many places the Education Gospel badly exaggerates the proportion of jobs requiring more schooling. In doing so, it raises expectations that cannot be met, and thus risks turning many against the very expansion of higher education that may be desirable.

Similarly, the Education Gospel has generally exaggerated the contributions of education to economic growth (Wolf, 2002). Levels of education are easy to quantify, so they have often been incorporated into the statistical work of growth economists. But a much greater variety of factors are responsible for growth including global economic conditions, national governing structures; the socio-political climate including its stability; macro-economic policies (fiscal, monetary, trade, and tax policies); institutional settings including financial, legal, and corporate institutions; structural and supportive policies including education, labor relations, science and technology policy; and regulatory and environmental policies (Landau, Taylor, and Wright, 1996). The remarkable growth of Asian countries, the decline of the U.S. in the 1980s and its resurgence in the 1990s, the varied fortunes of the European Union, the stagnation of most African countries, and the recent worldwide financial crisis are all due to many different factors. Surely, no one can possibly believe that the financial collapse was caused by the failures of education.

This over-preoccupation with education simply promises too much so that frustration with the educational system regularly boils over. The "let's make education better" mantra often means that public policies designed to alleviate social and economic conditions necessary for educational success are neglected. The result has been delusional goals and self-defeating efforts since educational institutions themselves cannot cope with the differences among students caused by inadequate housing and health care, poor nutrition, community conditions that make daily life an immense struggle. For many students in higher education, the pressures of work and family in addition to schooling lead to dropping out, and these pressures cannot be alleviated without child care policies, income support, and employment policies well beyond what educational institutions themselves can provide.

A worthy version of the Education Gospel would acknowledge the limitations of its current variant. It would avoid the exaggerated rhetoric and try to be more thoughtful about the pace of change and where that change is actually occurring. It would avoid "sloganeering," particularly by being concrete about the practices entailed in phrases like "lifelong learning" or developing the necessary skills for the "knowledge revolution." It would not treat education as the only solution or even the primary solution to complex social and economic problems, but would instead acknowledge that education is often *part* of the solution to growth, or social stability, or equity, or unemployment, and that other social and economic reforms are both necessary and complementary.

Similarly, the practices associated with vocationalism have had much to offer, but they too often take exaggerated and inequitable forms. The most encouraging aspect of vocationalism is that it has made formal schooling much more important. In many ways occupational preparation in formal schooling is superior to traditional work-based learning and apprenticeships, which suffer from endemic conflicts between production and learning, the tendency of employers to poach workers rather than train their own, and the inequities of family-constrained mobility. But in some cases educational inflation seems to be taking place with no benefit either to the individual or to society—for example when individuals fail to obtain work in the vocations they have prepared for or when individuals continue their schooling because alternative forms of preparation have been eliminated. While educational expansion is often positive, it has its negative outcomes as well.

As formal schooling has replaced on-the-job apprenticeships, it has facilitated the incorporation of new knowledge and new skills, including those based on research and advances in technology and work organization. Furthermore, it has brought new subjects into the curriculum, broadening conceptions of competence and bringing the outside world closer to the classroom than was previously true. The higher education system today is broader, more inclusive, and more open to change than at any time in history. Despite many limitations, higher education holds more promise for larger numbers of people and for its social and economic contributions than ever before, primarily due to its connections to vocational goals.

The down-side is that vocationalism tends to become unbalanced in the competencies it teaches. In some cases—particularly low-level vocational education and short-term job training—it has become too job-specific and thus often fails to educate individuals for work over the long term and for continuing learning on one's own. In other cases the academic slant of formal schooling has downgraded non-cognitive competencies like the visual and kinesthetic, important though they may be in life, and converted vocational and professional programs into academic exercises that are remote from the world, a complaint often registered by students. The version of vocationalism that seems most admirable is one that incorporates a variety of competencies, including cognitive *and* non-cognitive abilities, conceptual approaches *and* their application in different spheres including production, but that leaves job-specific and firm-specific skills to be learned on the job. These are balances not easily achieved in a world that tends to see things in either-or terms. They are balances worth supporting.

One of vocationalism's major contributions lies in transforming the potential for equity. The importance of higher education in providing access to the professions is certainly a major progressive step in comparison to the limits posed to access because of family status, race, gender, religion, political ideology, place of birth, and so on. Access is hardly free of these kinds of determinants and vocationalism has contributed its own forms of inequality through the differentiation of educational institutions that reflect various forms of discrimination and resource allocation. Still, few would call for a return to occupational access based on any other standard than educational achievement.

Yet another admirable feature of vocationalism is that it has expanded options in educational institutions. This has led to the incorporation of new subjects and competencies, to more dynamic and entrepreneurial institutions, and to an education system less inward-looking and more responsive to external demands—from students, employers, and the public. On the other hand, the policies that would allow individuals to take advantage of choice—particularly with respect to career choice—are typically under-developed. Too many students (and their teachers) simply do not understand the possibilities and the consequences of the available choices. This means that one of the things all students need is knowledge of the educational system itself and of the appropriate paths to different occupations, along with the acquired ability to make appropriate choices at crucial junctures. The expansion of choice and the consequences of choices necessary for effective and productive decisions depend upon such information. Distortions lead to negative consequences in an environment of expansive possibilities.

Overall, then, vocationalism has ushered in substantial advancements, particularly in expanding the roles of schooling, promoting both public and private goals, changing the nature of skill acquisition, enhancing the ability to address equity, and expanding choices and the flexibility of educational institutions. But for all these positive transformations, there are negative consequences as well. It would be good to expand the scope of positive consequences by providing a greater role for work-based learning rather than one that relies exclusively on school-based learning. This could be done by balancing the values of learning for its own sake with the values of citizenship and ethical behavior on the other hand, with an emphasis on vocational outcomes seeking greater equity through a variety of school and non-school policies. These are not simply nice ideas, but are essential in order to optimize vocational opportunities themselves, for it is all too easy to imagine a world where narrow work skills are all that matter and where non-utilitarian subjects like the arts and the humanities have been eliminated. A world in which educational institutions are limited to providing preparation for job-specific entry is a world where the great educational gains of the last century have been turned upside down because educational institutions have turned into mass producing factories.

Part II
Governance and Managerial Dilemmas

CHAPTER 3

Who governs higher education?

Marvin, the reason you are such a good
dean is that you think like a businessman.
(Conversation with a member of the University
of Pennsylvania's Board of Trustees)

No one really governs higher education. There are, however, lots of stakeholders, and various constituencies with high expectations and desires, who often act as if they were higher education's rightful governors or, at least, the governors of particular institutions. The constituencies vary in influence and power, according to the institution and the particular issue. But even the most powerful decision-makers at any given moment do not govern higher education. Still, if I had to choose, I would make the case that the most powerful decision-makers are boards of trustees and the institution's professional managers. The reasons are relatively simple: as market forces and capital funding have come to dominate universities and colleges, trustees with business acuity and corporate decision-making abilities shape educational decisions. As colleges and universities have come to resemble mini-cities, professional managers shape the long term plans and day-to-day decisions. Neither boards nor managers act unconstrained; they are almost always mindful that they preside over institutions that have educational responsibilities.

The shifting locus of power is in itself neither good nor bad; it comes with both attractive and unattractive aspects. It is real and influential, and needs to be included in planning and decisions about higher education. Certainly the shift is not going away, not as long as universities and colleges continue to offer a wide spectrum of services and claim to prepare students for labor markets. The higher education industry has become too big to run without constant attention to finances and to professional management. Gone are the days where planning committees are told "focus on what is possible and we will think about the money later." Not yet gone, but hopefully on their last legs, are rhetorical flourishes—I would call it blathering—about needing more top-down management and more efficient management structures or about the sacred division of powers embedded in the ideology of shared governance. Quiet and considered decisions with respect to goals and objectives are needed, and how to manage their implementation. The relationships between educational outcomes and governance are ambiguous and we will just have to live with that.

3.1 A journey of awareness

When I first decided to become an academic historian, I was convinced, primarily by my professors, that the faculty governed, for they did the research and teaching and had overall responsibility for the institution's welfare. Most of all, the professors protected colleges and universities from the intrusions of the outside world. Two of my Columbia University history professors, Richard Hofstadter and Walter P. Metzger, had even written what was the bible for their generation, *The Development of Academic Freedom* (1955), which made clear that the professors' right to pursue their scholarship and teaching in unbiased, non-ideological ways was the soul of higher education and the only security against the populist anti-intellectualism of American society.

By the end of 1960s, as I was finishing my doctoral dissertation, faith in professorial governance was harder to maintain. Student demonstrations around civil rights and the Vietnam War involved complaints that professorial neutrality and the non-biased, non-ideological approach to knowledge was itself ideological. Among graduate students new ideas about the social construction of reality gave intellectual substance to the criticism that professors were primarily interested in their own ends, that they lacked the moral fiber to stand up for what was right. Students were heirs of the university, and their voices needed to be taken more seriously than any others. This view, at least to me, was only partially successful in convincing me that students were important enough to take charge. And, when the students' concerns in the 1970s ultimately translated into freedom from *in loco parentis* regulations (why after all should universities and colleges have the right to restrain student personal behavior when their parents had long since given up seemed to be the common view), when the highest moral value became being left alone to do what they wanted to do, I was sympathetic, but such an outcome left the idea of students as governors of higher education behind. In the 1980s students would be identified as consumers, meaning they had to be sold education and satisfied with the results, which gave students considerable influence but not the power of governance.

For a while, the public became the potential owner, especially as the number of public institutions of higher education and the number of students enrolled in them skyrocketed after 1960. Carrying more and more of the costs of the rapidly expanding higher education system, it seemed clear that the public, through governors and state legislators, had taken over as the authoritative voice in higher education. The constituency that paid for the service owned the product, which seemed a simple truth of market economies. That turned out to be somewhat true, but in practice the public presence has been sporadic. The amount of money waxed and waned, and there were lots of moments when it seemed that public bodies and public regulations were going to take over, but higher education institutions seem to have myriad ways to preserve their autonomy. Despite the growing claim to govern higher education, public bodies have much better things to do with their time than manage colleges and universities. They intrude, but institutional autonomy remains the rule.

My own view of the dominant governing voices took a substantial turn beginning in the 1980s, with the emergence of two groups of powerful decision-makers: governing boards and professional managers. The power of these two groups, often working closely with one another, certainly more closely than with either the students or faculty, was quite extraordinary. Their decisions made clear that higher education was an industry, a somewhat unique industry in which education and research were important, but which depended upon and looked to constant infusions of money and economical and efficient management in order to succeed. How this happened is the story that follows.

3.2 Changing locus of power

I became dean of the Graduate School of Education at the University of Pennsylvania in 1987. At my first meeting with the university provost to go over the school's budget I was introduced to the provost's budget director, a person and position I didn't know existed, who proceeded to grill me on the relationship between my plans for the school and the financial numbers staring me in the face. His basic message is: you can't do what you want to do if you do not change the financial situation of the graduate school. Without the right numbers, your plans are nothing more than hot air. He turned out to be correct.

Other venues furthered my learning curve. Internal faculty battles over the outcomes of searches for new professors often took much of my time. Which of the final three applicants was most deserving of a job offer? The question went to the heart of faculty governance, of faculty responsibility and power. It was here that the concept of shared governance gave faculty the critical decision of who would join them as peers. The protests and contentions over faculty appointments, as well as promotions and tenure, often took on the character of mini-wars. Rarely did anyone state the obvious, that the differences among the finalists were usually minimal and besides there was almost no way to predict which ones would flourish as scholars and teachers and which ones wouldn't. The battles had to be taken seriously, in part because they were so divisive, but primarily because such appointments are one of the few serious powers the faculty still possesses.

Meanwhile I was regularly participating in meetings in other parts of the university in which decisions that determined the future shape of the institution were taking place, decisions that revealed more fully the nature of power and responsibility. At the University of Pennsylvania, they occurred in unending fashion. Should a new chemistry building be built? Should we renovate the university's landmark football stadium or build a new student center? What should be built on the huge parking lot adjacent to the main campus and how much of the new construction should be devoted to retail stores, private office space, or a first-class hotel—all ways of potentially expanding income? Expand the size of the School of Arts and Sciences or support the continuing growth of the Business School? Should one school be subsidized at the expense of another, one department funded disproportionately to others, and how large should the differences be? Should a neighboring hospital be bought and its medical school merged with the university's existing medical school and hospital? How should the funds from billion dollar fundraising campaigns be allocated? What should be the size of a tuition increase?

Although individual professors were sometimes participants in these decisions, faculty as a constituency was rarely consulted and if they were, the consultations were perfunctory, a *pro forma* tipping of the hat to older practices or codified rules that said the faculty must be consulted. When professors did complain, the complaints rarely came with genuine alternatives; usually the call was for more study and greater consultation, a kind of "let's delay while we talk it over some more." Such opinions were infrequently taken seriously, often being converted into "how do we get around the faculty complaints" by the administrators, professional managers, and board of trustee members. Claims by the faculty that they were the essential decision-makers in the university were treated as rather desperate pleas by professors to keep alive memories of professorial importance and the legacy of shared governance. In closed door sessions, administrators guided by the advice and information provided by professional managers made the recommendations. The information itself was often based on data provided by key members of the board of trustees, who in turn decided the future of the university.

Individual students were occasionally part of various decisions, but students as a group were thought of as potential problems easily gotten around. After years of student-based planning for a new student center, Penn's board of trustees decided that the plan should be shelved because it was too costly and the use of the available land rethought. Since the President and I, as Interim Provost, were in on the decision, I was then delegated to "handle" the students, which involved telling them that we were suspending the planning process to review the options. The student center plan was eventually dropped in favor of a new hotel, retail stores, and a bookstore managed by

Barnes and Noble that included a café to attract the students, which was a sign of what really mattered.

Another incident made clear how feeble the faculty had become. During a particularly difficult and controversial moment at Penn, following a series of racial incidents and the removal of the student newspaper from its distribution sites by a group of African American students, I appointed an African American professor of social work to review the event. His conclusion was that taking away the newspapers on the part of the African American students was a violation of the university's policies on free speech, but he also recommended that no punitive action be taken by the administration against the students and that an educational process of understanding occur on what free speech constituted within the context of university life. I agreed and the President accepted my decision. Key members of the university's board of trustees became quite upset. They were already angered by media reports, especially in *The Wall Street Journal*, chastising Penn for being too politically correct. Powerful trustees were determined to speak out publicly in order to separate themselves from what they viewed as the administration's excessive softness on minority issues—privately complaining that if the newspapers were stolen by white students, they would have received considerably worse than a slap on the wrist. However, the trustees also thought highly of me and the President, so we entered into quiet negotiations over a public document that expressed disapproval of my decision, a result with which the President and I could live. This was easily accomplished, the board's statement circulated and published, and the board and administration moved on. Indeed, so satisfactorily was this tempest put behind us, that the same board members who generated the document soon asked me to become the permanent Provost after a new President was appointed. (I said no. It was time for me to get out of administration.)

The university's faculty senate was not satisfied; its members were incensed that the board of trustees would dare to mingle in the affairs of the administration, for such behavior violated the long-standing tradition of separation of powers, the much discussed "shared governance," a tradition that in the faculty's view relegates the trustees to fiduciary oversight and fundraising. This tradition is something of a standing joke, one in which everyone uses the shared governance phrase without really believing in it.[1] The board of trustees took the faculty condemnation of what the board members considered a mild chastisement of the Provost and President in stride. Why fight over the past, especially when you feel secure that you (the trustees) have the right and the responsibility to protect the university from the misjudgments of the administration it appoints? Life moves on. But the lesson is clear: the board of trustees says and does what it wants, careful in this case not to provoke conflict with an administration it trusts. The faculty response is window dressing, a bit of theater, more or less interesting, but not especially important or significant.

Over the last few decades the rising power of boards of trustees and professional managers has become ever more evident. This holds for boards at public universities (or boards that preside over public systems) as well as for boards at private institutions. In numerous states the politicization of public systems has forced the ouster or resignation of Chief Executive Officers at the University of Michigan, the State University of New York, University of Minnesota and Missouri at Columbia, and overruled the administration at the California university system over affirmative action. While this behavior has evoked some reaction, more evident is that the trustees can and do whatever they will, with little serious hindrance. At public institutions, trustees, often speaking in the name of the governor and state legislature, claim they have a direct responsibility to the taxpayers, which overrides everything else. At private institutions, trustees speak of representing the institution's investors—alumni, students, philanthropists, and even the public, as well as the usual stakeholders—assert that they are the only ones who have the institution's total welfare at heart. Moreover, trustees have become exceedingly reluctant to serve as rubber stampers of administration decisions, especially sensitive to how those decisions will look to the outside world. Trustee activism, the sense of institutional ownership, has dramatically changed the balance of power within higher education (Chait, 1995; Chait and Holland, 1996).

For professional managers, the change has been dramatic. Between 1987 and 2007, staff positions in colleges and universities almost

---

[1] See, however, the powerful defense of shared government in Scott, 1996.

doubled, a rate much faster than enrollment growth and faculty growth. The ratio of staff and managers to students rose by 34 percent, compared to 10 percent rise in the ratio of instructors to students (Brainard, Fain, and Masterson, 2009). The numbers tell only a small part of the story, for the complexity of decision-making in what are increasingly mini-cities called colleges and universities has combined with a fascination for business-style management to make professional managers, with substantial expertise in complex and often highly technical areas, powerful decision-makers with substantial influence in governing board decisions.

Neither trustee activism nor managerial responsibilities are new in higher education. Activist trustees and governing boards have frequently in the past made university and college presidents' jobs extremely difficult (Link, 1995). But historically trustee activism was typically limited to grousing about student behavior, the rejection of applicants from the children of alumni, or the quality of football coaches. There were, of course, incidents which triggered more vigorous trustee interventions, as in the late 19th century, when professors were fired for their 'socialist' views, or during World War I, when anti-war faculty were forced to leave. During the McCarthy era in the 1950s and in the face of student demonstrations during the 1960s and early 1970s, the stakes escalated as boards accused administrators of being soft on lefties and student radicals. And as early as 1918, Thorstein Veblen published *The Higher Learning in America: a Memorandum on the Conduct of Universities by Businessmen* on the takeover of universities by leaders proposing to act like captains of industry. Even so, the assertion of board of trustee power as 'normal', as part of the responsibilities inherent in the job, as in the best interest of the institution was not the given, at least not in the sense that it was supposed to be that way.

Even today it would be a mistake to judge the overarching influence of boards of trustees as a victory over all the other constituent groups in and outside higher education. At most institutions trustees and academic executives work closely together. With the growth of professional managers in most non-academic administrative offices, especially in areas of financing, fundraising, endowment investments, facilities, student affairs, public and governmental relations, legal representation, and human resources, trustees are often working with individuals similar to those they manage in their professional roles. Presidents often find trustee assertiveness useful when they want to rein in out of control fiscal expenditures. Boards tend to seek ways to better the conditions for faculty and for students, for they rely on strength in both groups for prestige and in promoting their institution. And, for many board members, simply going to the occasional football game, eating substantial meals, and seeing old friends (often business and political colleagues) suffice; they are not looking for intense, stressful, public spites with the university administration, faculty or students. For many college and university presidents, that is just fine and most meetings of boards are pretty much as they have always been—tell board members all the good things that are happening, give them a problem or two to chew on, and send them on their way with the admonishment to raise more money—these are still pretty standard. Increasingly, however, that has not been enough and in the past few decades the level of trustee activism has substantially broadened and intensified and become more open and conflict-ridden, a phenomenon that has become more extreme as economic conditions have worsened. The long-term consequences for the governance of higher education are significant: higher education has become the domain of those who understand money, power, and decision-making.

3.3 Return on investments really matters

Governing board assertiveness goes beyond higher education, for the process has also been manifest in other sectors. Museums, hospitals and health-care systems, banks, insurance companies, entertainment and media industries, foundations and a host of non-government organizations (NGOs) have all seen greater activism on the part of oversight boards. Even where boards have clearly fallen down on the job, as they did with banks in the first decade of the new millennium, the call has been for greater activism and a less cozy relationship with executive leaders and management, a sign that trends of the last few decades will continue or intensify. Often pilloried for being gentleman's clubs that paid little attention to the institutions they oversaw, boards of directors in the 1990s and 2000s changed, in composition and in the rules by which they were governed. Boards of directors in the profit and non-profit sectors began to evaluate CEO performance and sought benchmarks to determine institutional success. As the events at the end of the first decade of the 21st century revealed, these assertions of board activism were too little and too late. If boards are no longer gentleman's clubs, they have still been too lackadaisical, too convinced that they understood all there was about corporate and institutional behavior to fulfill the fiduciary responsibilities and protect stakeholders. Their failures, however, have not changed the activist stance, but rather increased its degree and consequences. Institutional governance in every sector of the economy has been remolded in the last 20 years.

The significant period of change was the 1990s, when the consolidation of stock in America's publicly traded corporations gave unprecedented power to large institutional investors. Pension funds like the California Public Employees Retirement System, the New York State Common Retirement Fund, and the Teachers Insurance and Annuity Association/College Retirement Equities Fund (TIAA-CREF); giant mutual fund investment companies like Fidelity Investments and the Vanguard Group; insurance companies and banks; nonprofit organizations; and wealthy investor groups organized for leveraged buyouts began to assert major influence over corporate decisions. During the 1990s, these powerful investors instituted governance assessment procedures, forced executive dismissals, changed the composition and role of boards of directors, caused the sale of unprofitable units, and demanded mergers, all in the name of increasing shareholder value, even to the exclusion of long-held criteria like long-term corporate growth, worker security, and institutional stability. The name of the game was stock market value (Useem, 1996).

Investor activism represented a sharp break with the past. Although executive authority had been eroding for some time, under the impact of environmental protection, health and safety requirements, and anti-discrimination regulation, the fact of stock dispersion among many small shareholders historically gave corporate managers substantial authority in directing their firms. The growth of large investors, especially through the exponential increase in investment funds and pension funds during the 1990s, dramatically circumscribed this autonomy, forcing corporate executives to accommodate an aroused, informed, and demanding investment community—who in turn were willing to tolerate huge salaries, bonuses, and incentives to corporate executives who followed the mandate to take company stock prices higher. While business publicly complained—and still complain—about government intrusion and control, the real revolution came in the growth of power over corporate decisions by those who managed large investment funds.

America's corporations thus became engaged in a governance revolution. Those who manage investor money came to identify themselves as owner representatives with rights of governance, and they made shareholder value—a euphemism for stock market price—the defining criterion of corporate success. One of the surest ways to increase stock prices became—and remains—bold announcements of substantial job cuts. While the last few years have seen high profile attention to extravagant salaries, perks, and bonuses to those who lead corporations, the real revolution occurred in the boards of directors and their relationship to the goals of large investment funds. Higher education boards quickly adopted the activism and the search for increased stock returns.

Indeed, perhaps the most important trend in higher education since the mid-1980s has been the emphasis on growing endowments and returns on investments. Like much of the rest of America, the idea of saving for retirement—in the case of universities, saving in order to have funds in the future—got converted into investing at high returns in order to be substantially richer than you were before. The stakes were high as endowments in the 1990s grew, often by double-digit percentages annually. The rich got colossally richer, but every institution talked and acted as if it could become, if not rich, then at least affluent. Even with the downturn caused by the deflation of the technology bubble around 2000, endowments at many institutions continued to grow and checklists appeared showing which institution invested well and which ones did not. Whether one went up or down or had single or double-digit returns, the overriding theme was everywhere the same: return on investment. The financial crisis of 2009 had a profound effect on the universities and colleges, just as it profoundly affected the pension funds in which millions of Americans invested. But while the crisis made

investors wary of stocks and more controversial investment alternatives, the fact is that it has not changed the apparently inescapable
emphasis on getting richer through investing and the belief that
money is the most important goal. And, that means that those who
understand investing will continue to have a primary say in the
major decisions of universities and colleges.

3.4 Managing higher education's mini-cities

Perhaps the least discussed and least understood of the governance
changes in higher education has been the emergence of professional managers and their enhanced decision-making power. There has
been a logic to this, for colleges and universities have emerged as
mini-cities that deal directly and indirectly with huge sums of money and provide a bewildering array of services (Lazerson, Wagener,
and Moneta, 2000). This change has been both necessary and worrisome. Necessary, because it reflects just how complex managing
higher education institutions has become and worrisome, because it
creates a domain that is entirely separate from and more powerful
than the traditional academic one.

The phenomenon is relatively new. Twenty-five years ago little
attention was paid to the management of colleges and universities.
The faculty members who took administrative positions had short-
term aspirations; other individuals who served as "non-academic
administrators" were rarely noticed—and then primarily by students
complaining about the quality of services or by faculty members
railing against bureaucratic demands.

Today this has mostly changed. Academic administration has
attained a certain degree of respectability within institutions, with a
fairly predictable career path, from departmental chair to dean to
provost to president. Those in non-academic administrative roles
often come with managerial training and experience outside higher
education; they are in fact not "add-ons" to service the faculty and
students, but trained professionals with genuine expertise. They
possess skills appropriate to their domain—financial, human resource,
information technology, planning, fundraising, public relations,
legal, student life—and skills that are transferable across multiple
domains. Their managerial roles have become larger, more com-

plex, and more intrusive than ever before because the higher education industry has become larger, more complicated, and more
important.

Colleges provide a smorgasbord of services to a wide range and
growing number of constituencies. As institutions seek to become
better partners with their surrounding communities, develop more
effective uses of technology, and construct buildings for all sorts of
purposes—as well as continue to compete for students and faculty
and staff members—they become more dependent upon professional managers to deliver services. Market and political pressures to
cut costs and raise revenues, a fascination with corporate-style
organization and decision-making, and calls for greater accountability have led to increased managerial influence.

Campuses resemble modest sized municipalities, with an array
of public works, social services, and market-sensitive functions.
The managers of higher education's mini-cities preside over complex infrastructures that include security and police; real-estate
acquisition, management, and development; budgeting and finance;
legal services; human resources; technology and information systems; public affairs, development, and alumni relations; student
services; community relations; sometimes hospitals and medical
centers; and a host of other business services. And because the skills
required in undertaking these managerial and service activities parallel skills in other industries, the last decades have seen dramatic
increases in the hiring of people from outside of higher education,
with MBA degrees or experience in corporate, non-profit, and government settings.

Some college jobs—admissions officer, registrar, bursar, director of student affairs—are traditional. But even those roles have
expanded significantly. Admissions now includes bringing in students from other parts of the world, a hugely complex enterprise.
Student life officers went from providing relatively straightforward
services to becoming competent specialists who can negotiate con-
tractual relationships, answer legal questions, and deal with budgetary constraints. At the same time, their relationships to students,
faculty members, parents, and the news media has become more
complex as a heightened consumer orientation among those constituencies pressures managers to provide higher-quality services at

lower cost. The internet has further heightened pressures. Student affairs personnel are acutely aware that within minutes of an unsatisfactory phone conversation, e-mail, or SMS between a parent and child, they are likely to receive a complaint from the parent.

Even the attempts to restrain some of these activities, save money, and reduce bureaucracy—the goals of out-sourcing—have often themselves enlarged managerial responsibilities by requiring decisions on the exact nature of the desired service, assessing competitive bids, choosing the provider, negotiating with unions, communicating the changes, evaluating the services provided by external firms, and not infrequently terminating contracts when the private service provider proves to be too costly and inadequate to the job.

Many people in higher education, especially faculty members, still essentially ignore the service managers or begrudgingly accept them as necessary nuisances, viewing their responsibilities as ancillary to the real business of the institution. But such an attitude is foolhardy. Increasingly, faculty achievements are linked to managerial support, not only in the desire for clean and functional classrooms and labs, but also in the need for assistance in grant development, technology transfer, and online pedagogy. Faculty income, status, and working conditions depend heavily upon their institutions' success. Managerial power, however, threatens the tradition of shared governance and faculty members often have little knowledge of management concerns and not much interest in becoming service-delivery experts, and thus feel intruded upon when professional managers tell them what to do and what not to do. While managerial roles remain controversial and their costs are regularly being challenged (Brainerd, Fain, and Masterson, 2009), the need for them has become so great, that it is impossible to imagine them going away or their roles diminishing. In fact, their numbers and responsibilities will increase.

3.5 Are business and higher education the same?

The trends of the last decades are clear. Governing boards have assumed greater power and are more aggressive in asserting it. Professional managers within higher education institutions have greater responsibilities and shape an institution's day to day life more than the faculty or students. Does this mean higher education and business are the same? Yes and no, or in the words of a widely distributed Hertz rental car television commercial: "Yes, but not exactly."

Higher education does not like to identify with the corporate sector. Business expects to measure its bottom line easily—through profits and earnings and, if publicly traded, through stock prices. It can evaluate its product in the market place. Unions have very limited influence and until the recent incursions by governments, regulation has been more or less nonexistent. Business expects its managers to know what they are doing, to act swiftly when necessary, and to keep the profit-making goal clearly in mind. Business has a strong tradition of hierarchical decision-making, which despite the periodic fascinations with team-building and horizontal decision-making has hardly been dented. In contrast, higher education's outcomes are less easily measured, and whatever the corruption of shared governance, its tradition still has some influence. Faculty tenure and academic freedom provide permanence of work and freedom of expression virtually unheard of in the corporate world.

Still, if higher education and corporations play by somewhat different rules, the governance parallels between the two have become remarkable. Like the business community, higher education since the 1960s has regularly lamented its loss of autonomy, even though both sectors have been quite free to shape their respective destinies, at least until the financial crisis in 2008 and 2009 occurred, and even here long-term regulation does not seem likely. External oversight of individual firms, colleges, and universities has been the exception—high profile cases to the contrary—and that is likely to return with the economic recovery after 2010. Compared to the extent of federal and state investments in higher education, regulation has been modest and sporadic. As in the corporate sector, boards of trustees have existed to protect individual colleges and universities and to support the administration, a role corporate governing boards also play often to the detriment of their companies.

The ways higher education went about its business exemplified its autonomy, even as institutions complained about government restraints and requirements. Few phenomena are as mysterious as the still largely hidden admissions process and the awarding of lifetime tenure for faculty. Even the much-vaunted peer review system for promotion and grants reinforced faculty autonomy. The network of self-reinforcing scholars looks remarkably like corporate CEOs serving on one another's boards of directors, working to protect each other from the intrusions of outsiders who understand too little about the enterprise. The ideology of shared governance and academic freedom reinforced autonomy. The former articulated the notion of special expertise; the latter granted academic professionals a special kind of freedom.

Higher education, however, has never had complete autonomy. Given the mutual relationships between higher education and society—its certification of professional status, defense and health-related research contracts, its role in economic development and in influencing social policies—total autonomy was never the norm. The larger and more important higher education became after World War II, the less autonomy it was granted. As in the corporate sector, higher education's difficulties led to greater government intervention. What the federal financing of America's highway system were to the automobile industry and the federal subsidization of low-cost mortgages and interest write-offs were to the housing industry, federal grants for student fellowships, for campus buildings, and for research were to the higher education industry—ways of asserting each industry's importance to America's aspirations for itself. Political events also affected the norm of autonomy, as the Civil Rights movement and the anti-Vietnam war protests and affirmative action and Title IX mandates made clear. There have thus been constant ebbs and flows in the relationships between government and higher education, although on balance, colleges and universities, despite their frequent protests, had and continue to have substantial institutional autonomy.

In fact, the most substantial constraint on higher education came from the marketplace. Competition for students and resources drives individual colleges and universities, just as it does businesses. Higher education institutions compete for students, faculty, research funds, in fundraising and in athletics. Since the 1980s, published rankings of colleges and universities have intensified the competition, in ways similar to various consumer reports on the quality of every item that is available for sale. Like companies, institutions insistently affirm the value of their products and services. The creation of sectors within higher education imposes its own uniformity since a school cannot afford to look too different from its competitors: "We are a unique college but really not much different from the others with which we compete" is probably a good way of phrasing it.

Obviously, higher education governance changed in the decades after World War II. The increased role of federal and state governments through funding and legislative regulations required greater political sensitivity and an eye on Washington and state capital politics, as well as on the idiosyncrasies of federal funding agencies like the National Institutes of Health, the National Science Foundation, and the Departments of Defense and Education. I once discovered this personally in the mid-1970s shortly after W. Norton Grubb and I had published a highly controversial and widely distributed critique of the career education movement. I was invited to the University of Wisconsin, Madison campus to give a talk on education. Having been told that the talk was going to be widely publicized, I discovered to my surprise there were no announcements around the campus when I got there. Instead of being held in the usual auditorium for such events, I was taken through a series of tunnels to a small basement room where I gave the talk to a small number of people. When I inquired of a professor friend about this, he informed me, quite apologetically, that some state legislators in Madison had gotten wind of my coming after having read a New York Times news report on our article. The legislators were strong supporters of vocational education and had made clear that someone like me should not be invited to the Madison campus.

Greater dependence on alumni fundraising meant more energy and expenditures on development, dramatically modifying college and university presidencies. Older and more diverse student bodies ended the tradition of paternal administration. Administration itself became the preserve of specialists—legal counsels, budget directors, student services personnel, and a team of vice presidents to oversee the more efficient management of the institution. These changes were not imposed from the outside, although government regulations required somewhat different approaches to governance and management. They were much more powerfully required by the demands of market competition—for money and for students.

At the beginning of the second decade of the 21st century, the constraints from outside are growing, in part, a product of the stunning reassertion of governmental responsibility in the wake of the financial crisis. But the constraints remain much determined, as they have been for some decades, by the interplay between the marketplace for money and students, on the one hand, and the activism of governing boards. Oversight and accountability are themes that have resonated, with waxing and waning of success, for more than a quarter century. Whether through accountability demands to improve the quality of learning outcomes or to make institutions run more efficiently and economically or through the forced resignations of presidents and chancellors for failing to reduce budgetary deficits, governing boards have entered almost every phase of university life. They are not minding their own business because everything is their business.

The corporate comparisons are important. Many trustees are themselves corporation executives who are constantly in the business of "restructuring," of having to develop new relationships with government and major investors. Those who are money managers search, sometimes desperately, for new ways to invest and manage institutions funds. The view point is direct: colleges and universities have to be managed in the ways businesses have to be managed and they have to show income returns that allow them to grow.

Beginning in the 1980s, this view became particularly powerful, as governing boards of public and private universities and colleges added individuals who believed they could make their institution more competitive. They showed little patience and resisted accommodating presidential and faculty appeals to move more slowly or to take account of faculty prerogatives. They viewed colleges and universities as entities to be restructured in ways remarkably similar to those in which firms got re-engineered, downsized, fused, sold, dismembered, consolidated, and reconstituted. The fiscal crisis gave them even more influence—ironic in light of the financial disasters they helped engineer—as the necessity to redefine the financial and managing systems has become even more apparent.

Students and parents have for decades been reinforcing this kind of trustee activism, raising questions about costs, the worth of degrees, the commitments to undergraduate teaching, and the quality of the facilities available to students. The language of both students and parents has been dominated by and patterned after the language of investors: what do I have to pay (tuition and other costs) and what are the likely returns (jobs and income)? When the payments become high and the returns are uncertain, doubt emerges. When the returns are insufficient, through high in-completion rates or the lack of available jobs upon graduation or being fired after only a few years on the job, doubt turns to anger, further fueling the pressure to reduce costs, increase accountability, and tighten the connection between labor markets and higher education.

Colleges and universities, like businesses, have become consumed by the bottom line. The language of corporations and higher education are virtually identical: restructuring, increased productivity at less cost, accountability to stock holders/stakeholders, quality management, greater consumer satisfaction, reduced administrative fat, more expansive use of technology, a focus on core functions, green sustainability. Higher education, one of the nation's largest industries, is in economic trouble, just like its counterparts in other industries. The pressure to reorganize budgetary and governance structures is all-pervasive.

Take the development of multi-million and multi-billion fundraising campaigns. Over the last quarter century, success in getting people to give large sums of money and efforts to keep all possible donors affiliated to institutions dramatically altered the presidencies of universities and colleges. It also led to an unprecedented willingness, even necessity, to let the check writers be heard and to provide them with a constant flow of information and attention. These investors want the data, in ways quite different than previously, and they want to make judgments on how the institution is being run, judgments that are distinct from and sometimes in conflict with the judgments of the administration. Like corporate executives in contact with institutional investors—the CEOs of large corporations holding conference calls with large mutual fund managers about projected quarterly earnings, for example—university and college presidents engage in regular communication with major donors, many of whom serve as trustees.

This has not gone unnoticed or ignored. Higher education has its own culture of resistance. When professors are criticized for their lack of accountability, limited productivity, mixed interest in teaching, political correctness, and the sinecure of tenure, they are quick to see their prerogatives threatened by external intervention. Their defense is by now familiar: outsiders have only short-term budgetary interests; they lack expertise in making academic decisions; they are ignorant of how their financial and managerial decisions affect the research-teaching balance; they do not understand nor do they value the shared governance culture of the academy; and they are frequently anti-intellectual and hostile to academic freedom.

College and university administrators are forced into playing mediating roles, often with considerable ambivalence. On the one hand, they defend academic culture, the importance of research, and the legitimacy of tenure and academic freedom. On the other hand, they face the need for sharp budget cuts, are frustrated over the faculty's shell-like defense of its prerogatives, want professors to teach more, and (despite protestations to the contrary) they think wistfully of a more hierarchical organizational structure that gives them greater freedom to impose needed changes. Caught somewhere in the middle, university administrators have increasingly come to identify with their governing boards or, at least, recognize that pleasing or managing their boards is their most critical obligation. Governing boards have become their most attended-to constituency.

3.6 Leaping into the future

There is a certain exaggeration in my argument in order to increase the clarity of the overall picture. In practice, higher education is not primarily about conflict. Governing boards, professional managers, political figures, students, and faculty adjust to their competing and overlapping desires and reach compromises over what will and will not happen. Peaceful association exists, although often the result of what is left unsaid and without resolving long term tensions. Moreover, my stress on institutional autonomy would not be accepted by many within higher education, who over the last 50 years have seen increased amounts of oversight regulations, accounting requirements, and a battery of legal challenges over affirmative action, Title IX requiring gender equity, cost accounting for grants and other funds, the awarding of tenure, confidentiality of records, sexual harassment, and countless other big and small issues. While tensions exist between governing boards and university administrators, the fact is that trustee indifference, absenteeism, and a virtually unshakable allegiance to alma mater still prevails. Most boards are too large and poorly organized to assert effective control and are thus reduced to sporadic outbursts of resentment, to micromanaging a few decisions, and to hiring and firing presidents. The politics and visibility of public higher education tends to exaggerate instances of governing board activism making it sometimes seem as if governors and legislatures are in perpetual war with public universities.

That said, the changes in the power relationships in higher education that have seen governing boards and professional managers become the primary institutional decision-makers are real and they are profound. Governance has changed. Power has shifted to governing boards and to managers with long term consequences. The continuing transfer of power to governing boards will continue to take place, especially as power within boards devolves to small executive committees—a phenomenon well established in the corporate sector—with the result that a small number of trustees have greater power, can act more efficiently and effectively, and can focus even more on budgetary and political criteria in decisions. The close relationships between governing boards and professional managers that have evolved over the last few decades will increase, as they agree on how and what decisions should be made and share the same criteria for making them. With more and more college and university managers coming from business backgrounds or being asked to think like business people in their jobs, as has happened in the student affairs arena, the shared normative principles that have already taken hold become even more influential. This also likely means increased reliance in presidential appointments on "floating" academic CEOs, individuals who may or may not have had previous academic careers, but are now full-time in the job market for presidential jobs. Shortly after I was defined as an excellent turnaround artist with a heart, the board of trustee chairs at two universities asked me to accept presidencies—both unsolicited by me. Had I accepted, I would have been well on my way to becoming a traveling university president. In the higher education marketplace, five years in any single presidential office is considered a long-term appointment. The very nature of such transitions means that the individuals involved in them are people whose primary allegiance is to the governing board that appoints them and whose audience is the governing board that potentially might appoint them. They are short-term accommodators.

This has already happened at institutions where relations with the trustees guide almost every major decision (and lots of small ones) in presidential offices. The language of higher education decision-making is filled with a rhetoric imitative of corporate and invest-ment communities. In the 1980s, I referred to a million dollar budget surplus as "profit," for which I was chastised by a board of trustees' member, who said, "it is a profit, but we are not allowed to use such language in the university." The board member would not be so wary today of phrases like profit and loss. Indeed, university and college presidents have long become accustomed to being chosen based on commitments to restructure (i.e., do more with less people and thus smaller payrolls), consolidate and balance budgets, insti-tute efficient and cost-saving technology, and increase productivity. As the rules of governance continue to be rewritten, power shifts upward to governing boards with faculty lagging a distant second or even third in the face of market driven needs intended to please students.

One consequence of this has been occurring for some time: a growing focus on a narrow range of performance criteria for evalu-ating institutional success. Although harder to achieve than in the corporate sector, where institutional investors and executive man-agement traditionally have concentrated on shareholder value or stock market prices, it is easy today to imagine boards and profes-sional managers, with presidential acquiescence, making profitable bottom lines and higher student learning outcomes (as measured by standardized tests) the two most important criteria by which to assess institutional quality. Impatient with the ambiguities of higher education's tradition of multiple missions and believing that pleas to recognize complexity are defenses against accountability, gov-erning boards and professional managers could just agree to simpli-fy the evaluative criteria by which to gauge institutional perform-ance.

3.7 Resuscitating shared governance

There is, of course, an alternative scenario, one which is more desirable and substantially harder to achieve—the invigoration of shared governance among trustees, administrators, and faculty. The premise behind this is that universities and colleges are in fact different than corporations; that shared goals are more likely to result in productive actions; and that mutually strengthened parties bring greater strength to the institution as a whole. Resuscitating shared governance would give presidents greater protection from the most extreme demands of marauding trustees and would engage faculty with the professional managers who have become so crucial to every institution's success. Some presidents have begun to recognize this. Taking a page out of the trustees' play book, they are giving to faculty the same hard data they now provide trustees and that professional managers use, engaging faculty in their presidential cabinets, coaching faculty on how to talk with trustees and managers (the number of professors who lecture trustees and managers as if they were a naïve 18 year-old is mind-boggling), and bringing trustees, administrators, and faculty together in more honest ways than before, when faculty "show and tell" was the order of the day and consultations with faculty were more or less insulting presentations of what was already decided.

Invigorating shared governance will not be easy. Administrators remain dubious that faculty will use data to think broadly about the institution rather than as a source of proof that the institution neglects their needs. Some academic administrators are more reluctant to have faculty inside the organizational tent than they are about trustee decision-making. They worry that when provided with information, faculty will be primarily concerned with their own ends. This occurs frequently when overall salary data are shared, almost immediately followed by complaints from individuals over the fact they are below the average salary or not high enough above it.

There are numerous other difficulties. Professors have enormous difficulty defining and working toward common institutional goals. I do not know if the kinds of people who become professors are not ones who enjoy working together with others, or if loners who are professors find it easier than in other occupations. Or whether the structures of universities and colleges, with separate silos that make shared language and shared goals difficult is the problem. Still as one businessman who served on an otherwise all-faculty strategic planning committee told me, he was shocked at the individualistic nature of the conversations. It was, he said, as if the primary purpose of the institution was to serve each individual faculty member. Faculty definitions of shared governance too often tend to revolve around vetoes and resistances, complaints that the institution is moving too fast or that more information needs to be gathered.

Faculty governance is a network of committees with each committee frequently assuming that it has an obligation to stop any other committee's recommendations, creating a culture of distrust. Presidents and other administrators are frustrated by this, but they also use it when they want to postpone action or let something die, reinforcing the prevailing mistrust. (Administrators, of course, also do this with student initiatives, delaying action until the summer holidays have arrived and counting on subsequent loss of memory before the fall semester begins.) Shared governance in practice has unfortunately become a corrupt bargain designed to induce stasis.

These obstacles to a genuine form of shared governance are substantial but not insurmountable. One way to overcome them is to devolve decision-making to smaller units, combining greater autonomy with greater accountability. This requires increased data sharing, improved flows of communication (not simply more e-mails), and joint decision-making among trustees, managers, and faculty. It means ending the tendency to divorce budgetary considerations from faculty conversations about curriculum, teaching, faculty and staff appointments, and programs. And it means addressing serious issues too often kept off the table or relegated to the backroom, such as a unit's responsibility to balance its budget, whether tenure is necessary, new approaches to promotion or to appointing different kinds of faculty, greater attention to teaching responsibilities and assessments of teaching with consequences attached to them, and an end to faculty complaints about violations of academic freedom when they are told to teach on Fridays or prohibited from counting classes of fewer than 10 students toward their teaching load. Contestations over these kinds of issues will be difficult, but they are more likely to be resolved productively when they are conducted in units of manageable size with the power to make such decisions and with budgetary accountability.

It is a mistake to assume that trustee activism and professional management will whither away or that it is simply a good or bad thing. The threat to universities from the shift in the locus of power toward trustees and managers is matched by the healthy assertion that the academy is not so special that it can ignore economics and politics, consumer desires, and questions from and the participation by those the academy wants to pay for its activities. The shifting locus of governing power brings tremendous difficulties and stresses, but the outcome could be—and I emphasize the problematic in this—a system of higher education that is healthier for being held accountable, for being more articulate about what it does, and for being more engaged in managing itself.

CHAPTER 4
Managerial imperatives

Colleges have added managers and support personnel at a steady, vigorous clip over the past 20 years, new research shows, far outpacing the growth in student enrollment and instructors....[The findings] raise questions about priorities and provide fresh ammunition for critics of supercharged spending. Even before the recession, colleges were under pressure as students and parents reeled from tuition hikes, and policy makers questioned where the money went.
(Brainard, Fain, and Maserson, 2009)

Before I became dean of the University of Pennsylvania's Graduate School of Education in 1987, I gave little thought to managing educational institutions. University managers, it seemed to me, were people who could be more or less helpful and often annoying, especially when it involved students and my own research grants. Deans and departmental chairs could obviously be useful or not when it came to granting special favors, like extra time off to do research or providing small amounts of research funds and obviously in recommending one for promotion. Still the overwhelming sense I had was that both academic and non-academic managers had little to do with my daily life as a professor. Of university presidents and provosts, I knew virtually nothing.

Within a matter of months as a dean—without any prior managerial experience—I quickly discovered how naïve, even stupid, I was. The institutional managers were in fact shaping many of the most critical decisions in the university. Some examples:

– University planners were profoundly influential in determining capital expenditures and the campus's physical growth. Which buildings were to be renovated, what new buildings were built and where, were instrumental decisions that shaped what schools or departments had status and which ones did not. It was not always a zero sum game, but more often then not, capital expenditure decisions involved winners and losers.

– Budget managers determined the parameters within which everyone worked. The fiscal consequences of decisions being made by deans, as decided by those overseeing budgets, determined what academic units could and could not do. Faculty and deans could propose new professorial appointments, but final say was almost always shaped by budget managers, who regularly pointed out what the fiscal costs of academic decisions were going to be over multiple years and that these had a way of compounding annually.

– Student services managers oversaw an extraordinary array of activities involving large numbers of students and sums of money. The students themselves often felt much more engaged in these activities than they did in their academic work. Because such services were one of the university's selling points to incoming students, in part a product of the intense competition for students, the decisions by the student services staff were considered exceedingly important and they occurred pretty much independent of faculty and academic oversight.

– Development officers were crucial to the university's long-term fiscal success; even more so was the president's desire and capacity to bring in money. Since the university was in a constant fundraising mode—always starting, engaged in, or planning a new campaign—the development office existed as a permanent presence in the life of the university and in the life of every school and division of the university. The quality of the development officers and who they 'worked for' meant that some things got funded and others did not.

– Administrative staff made the implementation of every single decision, including every faculty decision, possible. What the staff believed were bad decisions or when the staff was not very competent meant that implementation could fall by the wayside. Without good staff in place, academic programs could continue, but they would be subject to continuing bureaucratic frustration.

– Legal staff, information technology experts, counseling and medical staff, research administrators, human resources personnel, and countless other service providers were quite simply crucial. The institution could not function without them.

Over the years, these early impressions simply got reinforced, and the quality of managers and service providers became a touchstone of my work as an administrator and professor (Lazerson, Wagener, and Moneta, 2000). These developments, as so much else in higher education, are worldwide: they reflect phenomena evolving almost everywhere. As Altbach, Reisberg, and Rumbley (2009, pp. 69–70) write: "A clear shift has occurred in government laws and regulations dealing with public universities in the last decade or two in many Canadian provinces and virtually all American states, in some European countries (notably the Netherlands and the United Kingdom), and very recently in China and Japan—all in the direction of greater managerial autonomy and flexibility. These efforts have frequently transformed public universities from simple government agencies into *public corporations*, giving the management new authority and sometimes corporate-style governing boards coupled with new accountability requirements. These new developments for greater managerial autonomy and flexibility—essentially moving toward managerial models associated with private enterprise—are collectively referred to as *new public management* and are designed to maximize the university's teaching and research outputs for the public as well as to provide incentives for maximizing nongovernmental revenue."

These developments in the United States and elsewhere have led me to a set of 'managerial imperatives,' challenges that every higher education institution has to fulfill in order to be successful. They are quite different than the usual items listed in reference to high quality institutions—the liturgy elaborated over and over of excellent faculty and excellent students. These are important, and I do not want to downgrade them. We are not talking about a tradeoff in which strong managers and well-developed managerial structures mean less adequate faculty and mediocre students. Quite the opposite; over the long haul a failure to take account of these managerial imperatives leaves an institution vulnerable to irregularities of markets in highly competitive environments. Meeting managerial challenges simply makes the institution stronger, more stable, and more capable of implementing what it wants to do than otherwise.

The most obvious way to phrase this is to say that many of the critical issues facing higher education institutions over the next decades will come in the form of leadership and managerial challenges that involve designing, organizing, and implementing change, assessing outcomes, and engaging in readjustments. These need to be viewed as continuing processes and not, as is too often the case, single decisions that are to be reviewed at some time in the future. The challenges require attention to institutional and organizational structures or else the intellectual, policy, and practical goals may well get lost or obstructed. It is a mistake, a terrible mistake, to underestimate the imperatives of meeting these managerial challenges.

4.1 The challenge of curriculum and instructional reforms

Overwhelmingly curricula and instructional debates involve some combination of intellectual and academic knowledge, considerations of the market for students, and political power. Each of these has face-value validity. That is, what students should learn and how they should be taught are intellectual issues, about what learning is most valuable and how instruction should occur, about the state of particular academic disciplines, about new forms of knowledge, and about the nature of integrating knowledge across disciplines or fields of study. In terms of curriculum and teaching, the questions are also about what kind of learning will be attractive to students or, in the case of professional education, what kinds of knowledge will best prepare students to enter the professional labor market. The third ingredient, which is recognizable to anyone who has taken part in curriculum and teaching reform efforts, is the way the debates and decisions are barely disguised uses of power, as in departments rejecting changes that will diminish their importance in the university or college. When the latter dominates, the most common result is stasis, at best modest shifts in the curriculum landscape without any substantial change. Overall, outcomes depend very much upon the interactions between faculty values and goals, the market for students, and the distribution of power within the institution (Cuban, 1999).

Less obvious is that whatever decisions are made by curriculum committees and professors, their implementation requires institutional leadership and managerial structures. Once a curriculum is decided, how should its implementation proceed and who should do it in what time frame? These are obvious questions, which are too often unaddressed in other than vague ways, as in "the new curriculum should be fully implemented within the next 3 years." What constitutes genuine implementation? Again, an obvious question usually answered by numbers of credits to be taken by students, and almost never answered by "we will decide outcome measures to test the quality of implementation." Who and how will the institution decide whether the changes in curriculum and instruction are improvements, achieve their goals—if indeed clear goals are articulated—or need to be further revised? Again, usually unanswered, because they are unasked.

If the above seems heavy-handed, it is, but not excessively so. The basic point remains valid: while curriculum and teaching reforms emerge out of multiple pressures and expectations, the managerial side of the process, actually implementing the decisions in a timely and effective manner, is treated as a side-bar, something that will more or less happen because the faculty says it should happen. Once the faculty decides, the process is thrown to administrators to manage and they in turn hand it off to managerial staff. There is nothing wrong with this; there is something horrifying in contemplating professors being required to manage curriculum details. They often have a hard enough time getting their course grades to registrars in a timely manner. What is wrong is the failure to acknowledge how important—how imperative—the managerial process is to the most basic of faculty decisions—what the curriculum should look like.

4.2 The challenge of serving students

The tremendous numbers of students and their increasing diversity, the large tuition charges leveled upon students and their families, and the now intense impact of vocationalism—the great expectations of jobs and fiscal returns at the end of the road—mean that students expect to be better served than ever before. How these expectations are expressed vary. They range from demands for smaller classes, better instruction, and curriculum choices more closely connected to labor markets. Further they want better access to high quality technology, career counseling, more modern classrooms and laboratories, as well as a host of life-style amenities like improved living arrangements, better food, recreational and athletic facilities, and countless large and small clubs and student organizations. What used to be called "the extra-curriculum" has now been renamed "the co-curriculum" to signify its heightened importance, which has been one of the most striking higher education developments of the last half century, leading to the creation of a huge, largely independent complex of student services. It is hard from the outside to imagine—and indeed even for many who work within higher education—how important student services have become to an institution's success.

What is striking about the development of student services is how little knowledge of them exists within most universities and colleges. These are not areas with which professors and even most university leaders are well-acquainted. Invariably, whenever concerns about an institution's finances come up, the almost instinctive reaction is to suggest cuts in student services, as if this was an area that had superfluous funds and besides, such services are seen as not being essential to the institution's mission. This is nonsense, since the idea of leaving the emerging and often complicated issues facing students to anyone other than trained student service professionals comes close to being ludicrous. Such a decision would leave student concerns in a kind of nether world; everyone knows they are out there, but no one really has responsibility for them. In fact, appropriate and proactive responses to student issues may well be a fundamental measure of the overall health of a university or college. If they are mismanaged, what students expect can quickly take on political dimensions in ways that neither serves them nor the university well.

Much of this was made clear to me through my efforts to change the relationship between student services and academic programs. At a meeting with departmental chairs in the School of Arts and Sciences, the largest of the University of Pennsylvania's schools, in my role as Interim Provost I expressed concern about what I took to be the lack of a serious relationship between the co-curriculum and the academic responsibilities of the university. I then announced to the chairs that I intended to develop closer ties between student services and academic programs, explaining, among other things, that I was hoping we could develop "living and learning residence halls" in which students could take courses and faculty might affiliate with or in some cases, live within these halls. My ideas were exceedingly well received and I was quite pleased with how the meeting was evolving, until a departmental chair proceeded to speak, as he said, on behalf of his colleagues, congratulating me on finally moving to cut the student services budget and to transfer money to the academic departments—which was not what I had in mind at all. In subsequent conversations with students I shared my ideas and got a highly negative response for exactly the same reason. The students assumed, like the departmental chairs, that this was camouflage to disguise the fact that I was going to cut the student services budget and give the saved money to professors. Unlike the departmental chairs, they were furious, in no uncertain terms, saying that the professors had little to no interest in them and that I seemed to be intent on destroying student life at the university. With a better understanding, I retreated from the front lines and proceeded to support others who somewhat later successfully implemented a living and learning program.

There are problems with student services and academic programs and co-curriculum activities are not one and the same. Student services have built up over the years in what often seemed like efforts to accommodate almost every request from student groups—somewhat like parents who would rather agree to support their children than face a confrontation. In the competitive world of higher education, any institution runs an enormous risk if it gets labeled "unfriendly to students." It is also clear that students and professors have different lives, different expectations, and the right to be free of one another. But the essential message is that student services are now an integral feature of higher education institutions, and they are sufficiently important to be taken seriously and managed well. That means well-trained, well-paid staff in the context of a well-run organizational structure. Anything less is, quite simply, dumb.

4.3 The challenge of research management

The research enterprise has changed dramatically in the last decades. While there are still scholars who work alone at their desks or in libraries, without much more than their computers and without research funding, they are a diminishing breed. The research enterprise is now driven by scholarly teams working across disciplines, across educational institutions, across national boundaries, and almost always with externally generated research funding—and the amounts count in the hundreds of thousands to millions of dollars. Accounting and auditing requirements, legal and ethical constraints, office and laboratory space, evaluations and reporting obligations, travel and equipment needs, technology transfer and patent procedures, and the complexity of keeping track of who is doing what and when have led just about every higher education institution with a serious research component to create an office of research administration, as well as every research unit having its own research administrators. The research enterprise cannot function without them. They are not going to go away, and they are likely to become even more important in the future.

Managing research goes beyond simply keeping track of things, however. External research funding, especially contract research with corporations and government or non-government agencies, almost always carries with it expectations that the outcome will be a product, and that the product will appear in a timely fashion. Failure to produce within the contract's deadlines or producing low quality products has consequences, from the obvious of receiving no additional money, to the possible demand that funding be returned. Researchers have their own stake in this. Who wants to be known as a researcher who either fails to fulfill the terms of a contract or produces shoddy work? The institution's stake may be even higher, since almost all contracts are formal entities between the higher education institution and the funding agency. The institution is at risk when money is squandered, behavior is unethical, or the quality falls below minimal standards.

All of this may sound relatively simple. It is not. Ethical, legal, and financial questions abound, and they rarely have simple answers or can be answered by non-professionals. When do the requirements of a research contract fall into the category of "secret?" Who owns the results of the research? Scholars with grants to write books almost always retain the right to the royalties, which come with book publications—provided the publisher sells enough books. But what about goods and products sold directly over the Internet, or in companies set up outside the university, which depend upon research done by professors? Higher education has always depended upon the free exchange of ideas. Corporations and sometimes government agencies seek to keep tight control over information, especially when they pay for it. Can university researchers be bound by requirements not to publish the results of the research for a certain number of years? Is the exclusive right to the findings for 5 years acceptable? Does 2 years make it better? If there is a possibility of financial gain from the results of the research, how should the university and/or the principal researcher or members of the research team share in that gain? The competition for research funding and status also means that the pressure to produce results is intense, especially when the funding comes from agencies that have a serious stake in certain outcomes as opposed to others. This too requires oversight, as scandals over data tampering make clear.

Serious questions are also likely to emerge about the status and income of well-funded researchers. Are they to be held to the same levels of accountability in teaching courses as non-research funded professors? Or is the system that research matters above everything else, or more accurately, that externally funded research matters enormously to the institution—for the dollars it brings, for the prestige attached to big grants—so that individuals who can amass such sums are disproportionately rewarded? There are already, in almost every higher education institution differentiated salaries—by perceived merit, by discipline or fields of study, and by level of externally funded research, with rewards that often take the form of summer research money or extra time off from teaching and other institutional responsibilities. These differentiations are fairly complicated and for many, they seem quite opaque. On the other hand, one could argue they represent relatively simple transactions: The differentiations primarily reflect some combination of talent, market leverage, and the capacity to bring money to the institution. Taken together, they tend to create a multi-track system in which there are losers and winners.

Among the many occasions this was brought home to me, one stands out. I was negotiating a contract to serve as the University of Pennsylvania's interim provost during a particularly difficult and controversial time in the university's history. The president offered me a salary to which I responded, "If I was the dean of the business or medical school, the offer would be much higher." His response was essentially, you are the dean of the education school not the business or medical school. The salary offer stands.

The issues related to research are obviously not simply managerial. As former Harvard President Derek Bok (2003) suggests, they are about the soul of higher education institutions. Externally funded contracts in particular raise questions about the very soul of higher education, what it stands for, what it is willing to sell, and what it loses in integrity by making the sale. But the managerial challenges do not go away just because there are philosophical and financial issues. Indeed, making sure that an institution does a research contract right may lie very much with those professionals who are not doing the research—their professional competence and authority to manage the process.

4.4 The challenge of money

Maybe it is all about money. It is not a far step to characterize what has occurred in the last few decades through the words of the song from *Cabaret*: "Money makes the world go round, makes the world go round." It certainly has seemed that way. The only thing that really seemed to matter was the money, as colleges and universities did everything possible to bring in greater and greater amounts. With costs rising, money became the engine of progress. For public higher education institutions, this was exceedingly difficult. Growing fiscal pressures on states from health, infrastructure repairs, primary and secondary education, prisons, and social services combined with growing numbers of students enrolling to strain state higher education budgets. This combined with a second phenomenon: the tendency to view higher education as a private good, that is, as something that benefited the individual who attended college or university and thus the individual should carry a greater proportion of the cost. The states reduced the proportion of public higher education budgets they had previously paid as well as spending proportionally less taxpayer dollars on higher education, while individuals paid more in the form of higher tuition and fees, as well as having to take out loans rather than receiving scholarships and grants. For private institutions, the calculus was simpler: charge whatever the market would pay, and provide enough scholarships and loans so that students would keep enrolling. The families would pay the rest.

The result of all of this was a spiraling, seemingly out of control, search for and dependence upon money. As a consequence, how to manage all that money became a major dilemma. Who would decide where the money would go? Who would keep track of what was spent and where? Who would file the reports showing fiscal accountability? Who would make sure the money kept coming in? The traditional pattern of pretty much reporting that the "money was well spent" or listing expenditures in relatively benign broad categories so no one really knew where it had gone gave way to much more rigorous forms of fiscal accountability. In effect, people who could bring in money and people who knew how to manage money, both in the sense of overseeing its expenditure and of investing for high returns, has become a defining condition of higher education institutions.

Although there is something distasteful about the hell-bent determination to have more and more money, in fact, higher education institutions are competing in a marketplace where they have to offer incentives to entice their constituents. For faculty, this means higher salaries, research and technology support, better working conditions, subsidized health insurance and pension plans—or during periods of financial crisis, simply holding on to what one has. For students, it means more of the things they already have at home or wished that they had. For staff, it means competitive salaries, tuition-free courses, and the same ancillaries that captured the attention of faculty, as well as keeping their jobs. The complexity of the financial system and the amounts associated with it require more and better professional oversight. Colleges and universities cannot do without it.

The financial crash in 2009 simply reinforced this reality. The loss of huge amounts of money—often amounting to 20 percent or more of annual expenditures—through deteriorating investment returns, sharp declines in state funding, and the initial resistance to raising tuition and other charges meant that those managers who know how to invest in depressed money markets, who understand how to cut costs and modify expenditure patterns, who can make judgments about capital investments and delayed infrastructure improvements, who understand how to negotiate new work patterns or to lower health care costs or to increase productivity became sources of gold, because their decisions can keep institutions from badly deteriorating or even, in the worst of circumstances, from closing. In prosperous times, those who understand the full range of ways to manage money are exceedingly valuable. In bad fiscal times, they become indispensable.

4.5 The challenge of educational quality

Deciding what constitutes educational quality is no easy task. It is complex and almost always controversial. Yet it has also become one of the major developments of the first decade of the 21st century. Taking on global significance, as higher education systems have been stretched to their limits by students seeking access, the notion of quality and how to determine what educational quality is, are becoming pervasive features of institutional life. As Altbach, Reisberg, and Rumbley (2009, Ch. 4) note: "Quality assurance has become a rapidly growing concern in a context of ongoing change in higher education around the world. At the same time, defining and measuring quality usefully has become more difficult. As the higher education landscape has become more complex, so have the expectations of individual institutions. In addition to educating, tertiary-level institutions have assumed (and been assigned) a broader social role—including resolving social inequities, providing appropriately trained labor, contributing to regional and national economic growth, and producing marketable research." What does it then mean to have and assess educational quality?

Like most such questions, it used to be easier to provide an answer. Certainly, in the decades after World War II, questions of educational quality were pretty much the prerogative of professors, both in the sense of individual professors creating and delivering their own courses and evaluating student work and in the sense of professors within a faculty or department defining the requirements for the major, diploma, certificate, or degree. Even though regional accreditation agencies have existed for decades, their focus on the easily measurable—books in the library, number of faculty with doctorates, e.g.—meant that in the crucial dimension of student learning, the professors reigned supreme. Tests of educational quality given by external authorities, as in state-wide professional licensing examinations in a host of subjects, in practice did little to challenge professorial authority to assess quality of learning. In effect, the professors created the curriculum, determined the requirements of each course, graded (or supervised graduate students who graded) the papers and tests. These were, by and large, the determinants of quality.

The trend of colleges and universities to more closely align their programs with labor markets, the growth in the authority of accreditation bodies to shape what a university offers and how it determines its success, the determination of government agencies to assure themselves that higher education funding is producing appropriate learning outcomes, and the tendency of students to "shop around" among institutions, taking a few courses here and a few from several other places (including internet courses) have greatly complicated the process of determining quality, and it has shifted some of the decision-making authority about quality away from the professors teaching the subjects. Professors still make the critical decisions; they establish the curriculum and students are primarily judged on basis of faculty-created and -graded papers, projects, and tests. But professors are now much more in the line of vision of groups and agencies external to the college and university within which they teach. They are more frequently than previously themselves being tested by the emergence of externally developed standardized tests or by internally developed outcome measures, designed to assess "quality added" or "performance indicators." In effect, these tests ask whether the students have actually learned something of what the professors have taught, and the tests may even be designed to determine what the external examiners believe the professors should teach. And, because college and university teachers are in greater numbers than ever before being hired on part-time and short-term contracts, making them even more vulnerable to external evaluations, power over the determination of educational quality is likely to shift even further away from the instructors.

So, what has this to do with managerial challenges? More than what might seem obvious. For one, these trends greatly complicate the roles of institutional leaders who have to become much more effective mediators between faculties and external bodies. This is especially delicate because increasingly external agencies are looking for more than tests of what is learned in classrooms, seeking to ask questions about the adequacy of professional preparation for the labor market or wanting to know how strong the students' communication skills, technological competence, and thinking capabilities are. Second, since the whole debate about educational quality sometimes looks more like a mini-war than a discussion, it has to be managed. That is, if colleges and universities are not to fall into nihilistic ways of behaving, with all sides acting as if they are surrounded by the enemy, then questions about what constitutes added educational quality, about how it should be measured and by whom have to be answered. They will not be answered simply by the faculty voting that such and such should or should not happen. Whatever the faculty decides will have to be mediated and negotiated with external bodies, will have to be refashioned into a program of action, implemented, and assessed, with the assessments leading to behavioral changes. The pressure to determine educational quality is not going to diminish, which means that the process described above is not a one-shot deal. It will have to be revised and refined and gone through multiple times. If all of this is not a managerial challenge, I do not know what is.

4.6 Managing information and communications technology

It is hard to think of a development that has received more attention, is suffused with so much promise, seems always to be on the edge of leading the revolution, invariably costs more than anticipated, and never seems to do quite what its proponents say it will do, other than information technology. It is absolutely necessary to the future of higher education, it opens up horizons on an almost daily basis that were unimaginable just a short while ago, including the capacity to reach millions of people around the globe and to make the vague conception of life-long learning a concrete reality. Information technology has changed libraries, redefined research, made borderless education possible. It has provided opportunities for administrative, managerial, and financial services to become more effective. And, yet with all the changes and the possibilities, most colleges and universities look pretty much the same, and information technology seems to function more or less as colorful lecture and class notes posted on a screen and as a way of managing registration, grading patterns, and the countless other forms of data required in higher education. In short, information and communications technology are most often used to do what higher education has always done.

Many of the possibilities and challenges of the new technologies go beyond a simple assertion of managerial responsibilities. For example, it is now increasingly clear that the capacity to pay the financial costs needed to create first class services is unequally distributed. Rich institutions can provide quality services; poor ones are barely able to provide basic computing services. To the extent that quality of information technology will have a substantial effect on people's lives, financially stressed institutions are under serving their students, and may have minimal opportunity to change that. While the resources can be managed to use money more efficiently and effectively, managers cannot by themselves create the resources necessary for high quality technology. That lies in the realm of public policies committed to diminishing levels of financial inequality. Managers can, however, apply what funds are available in focused ways dedicated to learning rather than the all too often tendency to put administrative concerns at the top of the technology agenda.

This need for focus is much more fundamental than most people, especially the modern prophets of expansive use of information and communications technology, are willing to admit. In the rush to join the crowd, almost everything gets put on the table. Student services require more and better technological applications, research requires instant investments, fiscal planning and financial accountability demand substantial resources, teaching cannot be done without totally wired classrooms and laboratories, instant communication is the heartbeat of every institution and organization, and just about every individual needs new hardware and software—students, staff, faculty. In the highly competitive world of higher education, everything is needed immediately and all at once. Indeed, in the frenzy it often seems as if the soul of the university or college is its technological resources. The result is what one would predict: high expectations and disappointing realities.

Leadership and management goals in all of this ought to be quite simple, at least in terms of articulating them. What exactly does an institution want, how will it pay for it, and who will manage the implementation? How will anyone know what works and, even more important, since very few things ever really work as planned, how can it be improved? In this, two things are quite important. The first is some integrity in articulating fiscal costs. I know of very few technology-based initiatives in which the costs were over-esti-mated—I actually cannot think of any. The reasons for this are not hard to guess. Costs remain vague in part because clarity about pur-poses—what exactly do you want to accomplish—is rare, and so money is spent in search of goals. Moreover, those who present the likely costs are almost always the same people pushing the project. If you want the money, you do not tell people how much it is likely to cost. Vague goals and self-interested promoters conspire to under-state the financial needs. Since this behavior occurs with regard to every information and communications technology effort, the results are vastly underestimated financial requirements across the board, followed by the search for yet more money or the need to cut expenses on the fly, both leading to little thought as to what really matters, and widespread disappointment and failed expecta-tions—which were themselves exaggerated at the start in order to get support for the project. And one asks why we so often have the feeling that the technology revolution just isn't getting the job done.

A second problem lies in the unwillingness of leaders to make difficult choices, especially ones that involve focusing on learning. Sometimes this has to do with the consultative nature of most high-er education institutions. Widespread consultation usually leads to "add-ons," that is, the process of simply adding recommendations to proposals that blur the goals and increase costs. Often the prob-lem derives from leadership's lack of expertise; most university and college leaders actually do not know very much about technology. But in the end, the real issue is that colleges and university leaders do not really think that learning is central to the institution. I know this seems paradoxical: Why else do higher education institutions exist? But the genuine reality is that the requirements of running the institution, generating revenues for it, and meeting the extraordinary range of responsibilities that currently weigh on higher education institutions, means that learning is just one of those things that has to be taken into account. But learning as the central focus of technological and costly investments? Not really!

4.7 Managing the managers

All of the above may sound like an extended call for more institutional managers, something that many within and outside of higher education find deplorable to the extent of outrage. One widely-held view is that universities are already over-managed, with too many bureaucrats whose primary goal seems to be to make life difficult for professors and students alike and whose presence diverts substantial amounts of money away from the institution's academic goals. The financial crisis of 2009 gave weight to this view and the calls to reduce the weight of bureaucracy and bureaucrats are legion (Brainard, Fain, and Masterson, 2009). The tendency of universities and colleges to hire increasing proportions of part-time instructors in order to cut costs further intensifies the attacks on over-managed institutions concerned only about money. The fact is that higher education is an industry whose constituent parts—universities and colleges—have to be managed if they are to survive and flourish, and walking away from that reality is naïve and quite stupid. The challenges described above make clear that more managers will be needed and that they are likely to posses even more power than they have currently. The challenge is not simply to add more professional staff in light of the demands placed on the institution by current and likely future trends, and thus giving substance to the complaints of bureaucratic institutions, but to look clearly at the genuine managerial requirements needed to lead increasingly complex universities and colleges. It seems clear that leaders in all institutions will need to take greater responsibility for overseeing their own managers, creating structures that might allow managerial professionals to become genuine members of the university community, a task of enormous complexity.

Part III
The Teaching and Learning Conundrum

CHAPTER 5

Academic disciplines, research imperatives, and undergraduate learning

*I would really like to teach one of the new interdisciplinary
courses in the general education program, but my
colleagues in my department would accuse me of
betraying my academic discipline.*
(Summary of numerous conversations with faculty colleagues)

For America's professors, the great triumph of the post-World War II era lay in the dominance of the academic disciplines. The disciplines gave faculty intellectual authority as they searched for new knowledge, trained graduate students, and shaped the undergraduate curriculum. Organizationally, the disciplines were centered in academic departments, which overwhelmingly controlled their own hiring, promotion, and the awarding of tenure, as well as becoming the most influential entities in the governance of individual colleges and universities. If all of this was insufficient, the academic disciplines lay at the heart of the research enterprise.

5.1 Purposes and tensions

After World War II, debates about the purposes of higher education came to the fore, with three themes receiving primary attention. The first came out of the immediate success of theoretical and applied research, as scientists who had been active during the war made an effective case for continuing federal investments in research on university campuses. Ultimately they were successful in creating the National Science Foundation and receiving substantially increased foundation support for graduate education and advanced research, preparing the next generation of scholars to expand the boundaries of knowledge. Indeed, it is safe to say, that university-based research took on an importance in almost every sphere of American life— what Roger Geiger calls, "research and relevant knowledge"—that had been barely imaginable before 1940 (Geiger, 1993, 1986; Graham, 2005).

The amount of money that became available for research was mind-boggling and with the dollars came a dramatic shift in the distribution of power as a *corrupt bargain*—my label—emerged. Individual professors able to gain substantial amounts of research funds achieved independent status within the university. The American system of distributing research money was usually based upon a peer review process evaluating the worth of the research proposal. While the money was channeled through a particular university, in practice, it was being awarded to the primary researchers, with the university serving as little more than distributing agency, essentially delivering the checks to the researchers. In return for this, the university received two things it desperately wanted—money and prestige—each of which carried considerable importance. Money paid professors' and staff salaries, allowed for graduate student fellowships, and bought equipment, but it also often came in the form of "overhead"—central administrative support, university libraries, heating and electrical costs—often amounting to an additional 50% of original grant. Money bought prestige and in turn, prestige made it easier to attract still more money. For the funded researcher, the university's gains were a godsend, leading the universities to treat research professors as treasures, who could, if they so chose, sell themselves to competitors. The power of money and prestige was simply too much for university officials, who usually chose not to look too closely at such annoyances as how the money was actually being spent, the actual conduct of the research, ethical questions involved in the research, the treatment of graduate students, the quality of teaching, or even whether the research professor was regularly on the university campus. Research funding created a free agency world, like the free agency of professional athletes, in which individual professors had enormous negotiating power—over salaries, working conditions, extra travel and summer funds—creating a two tier faculty system, akin to George Orwell's *Animal Farm,* in which all professors are equal, but some are more equal than others.[1]

---

[1] Derek Bok (2003) makes a version of this argument with regard to intercollegiate athletics and expresses worry that the same thing is happening with regard to contract research. My view is that the research enterprise has already achieved the power that now resides in intercollegiate athletic programs.

The second theme that emerged greatly expanded higher education's emphasis on vocational purposes, as more and more occupations sought to become professions through formal schooling, as existing professions extended the length of time necessary to enter them, and as new professions appeared. The increasing tendency to define the importance of higher education in terms of professional preparation had a remarkable affect on access: the route to higher income and status narrowed to a single-minded emphasis on going to college and beyond—the road to the American dream. No wonder that young people scrambled to get in, no wonder communities put pressure on political representatives to build branches of the state university in their area or to convert state teachers colleges into full-flung universities with graduate programs or to establish community colleges. No wonder that as the civil rights and women's movements took shape, they began to focus on access to higher education, laying the basis for the politically controversial affirmative action programs of the 1970s and 1980s. And, with entry into the growing number of professions becoming the dominant concern of students, came a revolution in the curriculum, with more and more courses and majors being established that claimed to provide practical returns.

The third theme in the debate about the purposes of higher education centered on general education. The movement for general education stressed a common core of learning, a turn against the tide of curricular fragmentation and disciplinary specialization that had already become apparent. General education drew upon 19th century traditions of the liberal arts and the belief that knowledge had moral and humane ends. World War II reinforced these views as general education took on the mantle of teaching common social values. General education's aim after the war was nothing less than preparing intelligent citizens capable of making wise and moral judgments in a world that had become increasingly dangerous. If America's colleges and universities, the argument went, could not recognize how important were commitments to and responsibility for maintaining a democratic society, what value did they really have (Sloan, 1980)?

5.2 The neglect of learning

The purposes of higher education that emerged after World War II
—research, vocationalism, and civic education—were neither new
nor were they easily compatible. Seeking to achieve them created
innumerable tensions. Yet each of the purposes expanded, although
in different ways. General education found a home on probably half
of America's colleges in the 1950s (Sloan, 1980), and continued to
be a feature of higher educational institutions around the country,
regularly debated and resurfacing in various forms. Research and
vocationalism became the essential features of American higher
education. As different as the two goals seemed, they had something in common, for each pointed higher education toward a greatly expanded curriculum to accommodate the desires of the faculty
and the goals of the students. Debates about purposes inevitably
drove faculty into questions of curriculum. What is the curricular
content of an education for citizenship? What should be the relationship between the liberal arts and vocational or professional preparation? How should research and graduate education connect to the
undergraduate curriculum? What should be the balance between
required courses and electives? What defines a major?

Often faculty questions about purposes became questions about
curricular modifications and departmental power rather than about
knowledge and learning. For instance, what courses should students take? When should they take them? How many courses can
students choose and from what menu? What should students read?
Do interdisciplinary courses water-down the curriculum? Ironically, what was supposed to be an effort to connect the purposes of
higher education to what students should learn, understand, and
make meaningful, converted into decisions about what each department would require of its students, into negotiations over how much
each department had to "service" (a commonly used phrase) general education courses, and into a fixation by individual faculty members on the courses they had to teach and their course reading lists
(Cuban, 1999).

During these debates, little attention was paid to learning itself,
how students learned, what kinds of knowledge they acquired and
how long they retained it, how applicable the knowledge was for

students' lives, or whether the methods of teaching and of assessing student learning were the best ones available. Curriculum was of central importance to professors since most spent their time teaching and put substantial efforts into reading lists and testing students' course knowledge. Yet learning itself and the appropriate pedagogy were rarely addressed, beyond students fulfilling course requirements and professors preparing lectures and seminar notes. The few studies undertaken to assess the impact of teaching on student learning had little effect on how professors went about their business.

Not until the widely publicized decline in SAT scores in the late 1970s did the question of learning begin to occupy a noticeable place in higher education, and even then the initial reaction was to blame forces external to postsecondary education—low academic standards in elementary and high school, too much time watching television or, what came later, playing computer games, even the breakdown of the family—or to complain that open and low college admission requirements had reduced student incentives to learn. Academia itself did not take seriously questions about the relationship between what was taught and how it was taught on the one hand, and student learning on the other. Only with the challenges to higher education in the late 1980s over the price-returns squeeze—soaring tuition increases and growing costs—did student learning become a serious agenda item, especially as public and political criticisms of the amount and quality of teaching mounted.

The faculty's concerns with learning and teaching have inevitably been translated into questions about what to teach and when to teach it, questions which were primarily answered within the academic departments and in terms of each academic discipline. What constituted the discipline's most important scholarly questions? What were the discipline's most appropriate methodologies? What were the cutting edge specializations within the discipline and could the faculty teach them? These were useful and relevant questions, but they were not about issues of student learning.

It is not hard to explain the relative absence of discourse within higher education over student learning or of any sustained discourse on the effectiveness of courses or about how well students comprehended what they had been taught (Association of American Colleges, 1985; Wagener, 1989). Little incentive existed for faculty and administrators or, for that matter, parents and students to worry about what students learned. As long as the system grew in numbers and wealth and everyone presumed that professional success and income returns were tied to college graduation, the breadth, depth, and content of classroom learning took a distant second place. And with faculty focused on their own disciplines—on their capacity to understand and teach the primary questions of their discipline—they saw little need to ask questions about the relationship of student learning to citizenship or vocational responsibilities.

There was a second reason why student learning was so little addressed. Classroom teaching became associated with academic freedom. What professors did inside the classroom had to be defended against external threats—from McCarthyism, conservatives and religious fundamentalists, leftist radicals, politicians, administrators, and ultimately from the students themselves. The defense of academic freedom had the effect of making the classroom a "private" domain—as the widespread faculty disregard of student evaluations often made clear. Any questions about what happened in the classroom, even whether students were learning anything, were viewed as threats to the faculty member's liberty. The transactions of the classroom, teaching and learning, needed to be excluded from serious observation and evaluation.

Instead of concentrating on learning, American higher education focused on organizing academic content and delivering it. Colleges experiment with technology and new approaches to teaching even less than elementary and secondary schools do. Sad to say, the recent versions of this, like the use of power point presentations, comes across as pathetic, usually little more than lectures with the lights dimmed so that the students can read the slides and enjoy the occasional animated features. Lectures and seminars dominate the presentation of knowledge, with the former often directed at large numbers of students. After the 1960s greater informality between faculty and students occurred with professors and students similarly dressed and referring to each other by first names. Informality may have enhanced collegial feelings between professors and students, but it led neither to students learning more nor to any substantial change in the delivery of information to students.

The lack of interest in pedagogical experiments reflected the dominance of substantive academic content over instructional values. The ascendant model of academic knowledge derived from the research universities. It was regularly contested, as evidenced by the various efforts to introduce specially constructed general education courses or to involve students in hands-on clinical or practical experiences or most recently in community-based service learning. Yet the dominant notion of higher education's knowledge base has remained: students should learn what the professors know and the most important kind of knowledge professors know is conditioned by the research community and its disciplines. Whether through departmental structures, the organization of course catalogues, reading lists, or the requirements for majors, the patterns set by the research universities have become standard for most of higher education, especially as research universities became the source of the overwhelming number of professors in higher education. Alternatives continued to exist, but they were precisely that, alternatives to the dominant pattern of belief and practice.

This argument, of course, risks generalizing developments at the research universities into what is characteristic for all of higher education, reducing the distinctions between liberal arts colleges, comprehensive universities, and community colleges to mere caveats. That is not my intention. Sectors of higher education and individual campuses differ, often in substantial ways. Nonetheless, I am persuaded that in the organization of knowledge and its relationship to student learning, the research universities have come to dominate the discourse and remain the most influential model. To quote Richard Freeland (1992, p.118), "The central tenet of this model was that the university whose faculty was most productive in research, as measured by publications in important scholarly outlets and... by success in attracting outside funding, was the best university. The model incorporated a clear hierarchy of values: it celebrated modern, scientifically oriented research above traditional forms of interpretive or synthetic scholarship; investigation of basic problems above applied work and therefore the arts and sciences above professional fields; research over teaching; and graduate-level training above undergraduate education. It also retained more traditional indicators of academic prestige: selective admission policies, residential facilities, and strength in the liberal arts and the elite professions... by becoming research universities, leading institutions altered the terms in which other campuses, occupying positions of lesser prestige, understood the requirements of upward academic mobility." Freeland's summary statement written in the early 1990s needs revision; contract and therefore applied research, professional education, and fundraising as distinct from research grants have all assumed substantially greater influence throughout higher education. The main thrust of Freeland's analysis nonetheless remains accurate.

Higher education's curriculum underwent broad, substantial change after 1970. Its size exploded and it became chaotic. Even small colleges produced course catalogues that made any notion of a focused curriculum anachronistic. Large schools had city telephone-book-sized course catalogues; as early as 1975 Cornell University needed 700 pages to present its undergraduate course offerings (Rudolph, 1977, p. 1). It was not anarchy, since some requirements continued at almost every institution, but the orderly progression of courses from freshman- to senior-level that had previously constrained choices and demanded that majors in a discipline go through a set of hierarchically ordered courses, from introductory surveys to more specialized advanced seminars, gave way. By the 1980s the range of what a student could choose to satisfy degree requirements, the very quantity of courses offered, and the difficulties in distinguishing between elementary and advanced courses were frequently overwhelming. And, as increasing numbers of students began taking courses at more than one institution or began adding internet courses to the dossier, the idea of an even partially coherent curriculum simply disappeared.

At the same time higher education accepted and even exaggerated the growth of the parallel curriculum in which student life flourished. Building upon a tradition of student interests separate from the academic interests of the faculty, colleges and universities increased the number and intensity of student services, built student centers, expanded residential facilities, provided health care and career counseling, supported an increasing number of clubs, and in many cases, created a mega-sized intercollegiate athletic juggernaut that frequently defined the image of what a university was about. Much of the justification for student life once asserted itself through the view that such activities aid students in learning the teamwork, cooperation, leadership, and responsibility that will make them more effective professionals and citizens, implying that academic learning contributes a modest amount, at best, to these goals. Its value has also gotten a huge boost from the recognition that many students need academic, social, and psychological supports that either cannot or should not be met by professors. As competition for students grew and as the student life itself became fragmented into highly specialized clubs and activities, student services became a place where almost anything was justifiable. So powerful had the extra-curriculum become that by the last decades of the 20th century, it was routinely being referred to as the co-curriculum, an extraordinary recognition of its role. Although efforts have emerged to bring the co-curriculum into closer connection with the academic curriculum—e.g., through living and learning experiments—the co-curriculum remains a parallel and separate domain, by and large predicated on the absence of faculty to the mutual satisfaction of students and professors.

These developments were tied both to the triumph of the faculty as the principals in higher education and to the power of students to achieve their demands. For the faculty, the dramatic explosion in courses opened the way for professors to teach their specializations, to make what students should study congruent with what the faculty wanted to teach, which was their academic disciplines and their methodologies. The students gained expansive choice in what courses they took and a robust student life in which they could engage. While Americans committed themselves to the extraordinary growth of higher education for all sorts of reasons—national defense and economic development, an educated citizenry, local and regional pride, personal income and vocational gain, the expansion of educational opportunity—the professoriate made the academic disciplines the organizational center and intellectual heart of universities and colleges. The students, with active institutional support, created a parallel and largely independent world.

5.3 The separation of science and morality

The triumph of separate tracks, with professors as master of their
domain, while students had wide choices within the curriculum
and were free to pursue student life free of academic oversight,
was not *de novo*. It did not just happen after 1945. It had been
evolving since the late 19th century, as the disciplines made scientific research and the methodology of science their *raison d'etre*,
creating a world that was by and large separate from that of students.[2]

For most of the 19th century, American higher education assumed
that the unity of truth combined science and religion in the service
of one another and that religion was the basis of morality. Higher
education's purpose was to reinforce this unity, training simultaneously the intellect and moral character. The curriculum exemplified
this, making the connection explicit in a culminating course in
moral philosophy, in which students explored the literature of philosophy and theology to confirm their obligations to family, community, nation, and God and to reconcile religion and secular studies. As universities and colleges became connected to national and
regional interests and to economic development—marked at the
federal level by the Morrill Acts of 1862 and 1890, which explicitly
articulated the utilitarian aims of higher education—criticism of the
curriculum's neglect of modern and practical subjects mounted, as
did the failure to offer advanced instruction and the limitations that
theology placed on scientific research. Colleges developed a much
broader set of purposes than the traditional one of preparing for the
learned professions and public life. New private universities—like
Johns Hopkins, Cornell, and Chicago—and older ones—Harvard,
Columbia, and Pennsylvania—as well as state universities like
Wisconsin, Michigan, and California at Berkeley capitalized on the

---

[2] The section that follows depends heavily on Reuben (1996), which shows
how colleges and universities redefined their traditional responsibilities
for the moral and character building of students to accommodate the
new expectation that the faculty's primary role was to become research
scholars. Reuben also argues, as I do, that the growth of the extra-curriculum was directly connected to changes in the organization of knowledge and the emphasis on research.

intensified interest in utilitarian and vocational outcomes, advanced research, and science to become the dominant players in higher education, even as the liberal arts colleges both adjusted to the new climate and justified their more traditional ethical and community responsibilities (Geiger, 1986, 1995; Leslie, 1992).

Initial strategies to reform the curriculum and to advance research tried to reaffirm the traditional connection between religion and science and thus between higher education and morality. The generation of "great university presidents"—Charles William Eliot (Harvard), Daniel Coit Gilman (Johns Hopkins), Andrew White (Cornell), William Rainey Harper (Chicago), and Nicholas Murray Butler (Columbia)—assumed that scientific research would continue to support religion. They hoped to show this by making religion a focus of scientific study. They failed.

By the first decades of the 20th century, efforts to put universities at the service of the moral goals of the classical college while advancing knowledge were in retreat, "the ideal of the unity of truth did not seem plausible to younger intellectuals trained in the new universities" (Reuben, 1996, pp. 3–4). Over the next decades academics came to embrace the separation of facts and values. Facts were what natural and social scientists discovered. Teaching values and having them implemented behaviorally was neither the responsibility of scholars nor the goals of classroom instruction. While liberal arts colleges continued to hold to the validity of morally-based instruction and responsibilities, a new generation of university faculty severed the connection between their search for knowledge and moral behavior, between their roles as professors and the institution's responsibility for student values and behavior. It was not simply the making of the modern university; it was a revolution that worked a fundamental change in American higher education.

By the 1930s, the dominant view of knowledge centered around research in the academic disciplines, structurally organized within academic departments. The advancement of knowledge occurred most effectively and successfully when it was specialized, experimental (controlled as much as possible), quantitative, had replicable methodologies, and sharply distinguished between "pure" and "applied" research (with the former accorded higher status than the latter). Most powerfully, knowledge was best acquired and was most trustworthy when scholars removed ethical concerns from their research, achieving ethical neutrality or ethical detachment. Only then could scientific credibility be achieved; only then could research achieve stature and social influence.

There were degrees and differences with which these views took hold. They were held and implemented most insistently in the natural sciences, which took seriously the need to separate research from religion and morality. But the new ideology came to dominate the social sciences also. Sociology, for example, saw the rise of a new scientism, in which facts had to be measured. The direct application to and involvement in social reform by social scientists was rejected, a phenomenon that at the University of Chicago pitted women faculty in a losing battle with their male counterparts for control over the social science disciplines (Bannister, 1987; Fitzpatrick, 1990). The humanities initially proved highly resistant to the separation of morality and science. The New Humanists critiqued the methodologies of science and its assumptions of progressive modernity. Potentially overwhelmed by the success of their social science and natural science colleagues, faculty in the humanities challenged the value and validity of morally neutral research and teaching. Among college and university administrators, few, if any, were willing to dispense with the view that an undergraduate's character and morality were an institutional responsibility. In the liberal arts colleges, the separation of fact and value, of science and morality, was especially contested (Leslie, 1992).

By World War II universities had made a substantial shift to viewing science as a value-free enterprise engaged in by ethically neutral researchers. If teaching needed to acknowledge moral and normative values, if the institution had to provide for the character-building of undergraduates, so be it. Outside of courses that examined, scientifically, such issues, these were not the faculty's problem, since they were best taken up outside the realm of scholarship, except insofar as moral issues were themselves a subject of scientific research. In opposition, many liberal arts colleges and those in universities that wanted their undergraduate program to be more traditional sought to overcome the disjuncture between the faculty as scholars and the moral responsibilities of teaching by urging required courses in the humanities and social sciences, as in Columbia's required Contemporary Civilization courses, in order to promote citizenship education. Administrators, unwilling to challenge directly the faculty's freedom to specialize and to engage in research, stressed the importance of teaching and faculty advising, as well as the faculty members' moral character—the professor as personal model. They stressed the importance of the humanities in keeping open the dialogue between scholarship and morality (not incidentally, making the English department the academic home of such concerns). And, wherever they could, universities and colleges expanded on-campus housing and gained institutional oversight of the extra-curriculum. Ultimately, however, higher education settled upon a dual track educational program.

One track involved the formal organization of knowledge—the curriculum—controlled and delivered by an increasingly powerful faculty. The second track—the extra-curriculum—was the students' domain loosely coordinated by student life professionals. While college and university administrators regularly stressed the complementary and overlapping nature of the curriculum and the extra-curriculum, leading the latter to be renamed the co-curriculum, the stress was more rhetorical than real. On university campuses the two curricula existed as independent and non-collaborative enterprises. In the liberal arts colleges, professors were asked to and often did breach the divide, although the trend was always toward separation. After World War II, the divide would achieve its apotheosis.

5.4 Triumph of methodology

The enlargement of faculty authority within the research and teaching domains was of extraordinary importance in the history of American higher education. Its story after World War II tends to be told as if this was a natural extension of the knowledge explosion and the potential contribution of knowledge to the national interest, stimulated by federal investment and institutional competition for prestige and dollars. But it is also useful to think of what happened in terms of the triumph of disciplinary methodology. Teaching a discipline to undergraduates meant training them in the methodologies relevant to that discipline. What this meant varied by each discipline, but in every field the pressure was toward a model of greater scientific methodological precision, a trend that had the effect of inhibiting the conversation between disciplinary scholars and their undergraduate students, who were interested in many things, with methodology not being one of them.

The evolution of research methodology as the driver of teaching and learning had been underway for some time, but the dramatic acceleration of efforts to achieve methodological precision after World War II was not entirely predictable. The early postwar years after all witnessed a tremendous outpouring of rhetoric about higher education and democracy, the importance of general education for an informed citizenry, equality of opportunity, and the utilitarian and practical purposes of postsecondary schooling—a sufficiently broad set of aims which could have tolerated substantial diversity in the organization of knowledge. In retrospect, however, there was an eerie duality about the aspirations of the academy and the rhetoric of democracy. On the one hand, democratic and utilitarian purposes gave enormous boost to higher education's postwar growth. The combination of knowledgeable and productive citizens and the application of science to economic growth and national defense was irresistible. It was precisely this engagement with the outside world, the successes that were palpable, which brought millions of students and dollars into the industry. On the other hand, the faculty sought to sharpen the academic disciplines' foci and to create methodological forms that separated their work from the citizens they were educating. The faculty, which in fundamental ways depended upon the postwar expansion of enrollments, was disinclined to make much accommodation to the calls for civic-minded education and the reality of greater student diversity. Even as the enterprise of higher education expanded, and even as higher education claimed utilitarian responsibilities—justifying investments in it and expanding enrollments—the knowledge that was being taught within the academic disciplines became narrower and narrower, more and more based on methodologies, and more and more disconnected from the everyday world of the students (Bender, 1997).

The way of the faculty had considerable merit. Given the organization of knowledge into academic departments based on the disciplines and the incentives to contribute to new knowledge, scholars were wise to construct technically grounded methodologies, with which they earned a distinctive status among their colleagues. The bind professors faced would have been difficult to resolve in the best of circumstances, for they were asked to speak to communities outside the academy as part of their civic and utilitarian responsibilities, yet simultaneously were expected to create a distinctive community of discipline-based colleagues whose language gave them exclusionary status. Mostly, they opted for the latter. In the historian Thomas Bender's words: "In retrospect it appears that the disciplines were redefined over the course of the half-century following the war: from the means to an end [civic responsibilities] they increasingly became an end in themselves, the possession of the scholars who constituted them. To a greater or lesser degree, academics sought some distance from civics. The increasingly professionalized disciplines were embarrassed by moralism and sentiment; they were openly or implicitly drawn to the model of science as a vision of professional maturity. The proper work of academics became disciplinary development and the training of students for the discipline" (Bender, 1997, p. 6).

Put differently, when faculty in the 1940s debated the curriculum and its relationship to society, they were engaged in discussions about an educated citizenry and the best forms of knowledge to connect their students to their post-college lives. This was the essence of the debates over general education and vocationalism. By the early and mid-1960s, curriculum discussions among the faculty—even with growing controversies about "relevance"—were much more likely to be about how to provide a structured introduction to each academic discipline. Undergraduate education was less about faculty concern for knowledgeable citizens and more about the specializations of each faculty member or department.

The extraordinary growth of higher education produced an enormously expansive industry built upon a shaky foundation, shaky because the foundation was held together by two critical conditions. The first assumed that economic returns to students would grow, opportunity costs would continue to go down, and students (and their parents) would always feel satisfied that each year of college was an excellent investment. As long as these occurred, the actual classroom enterprise made only modest difference. What happened when professors and students met in the classroom was not all that consequential as long as there was substantial profit in acquiring the degree. The second condition was related to the first: higher education depended upon the success of the extra- or co-curriculum to provide students with the learning students considered most relevant to their success—social skills, leadership, networking, knowledge of the world around them, community and civic participation. As long as the co-curriculum was well supported and thriving, classroom learning was just not that important. When questions got raised in the 1980s and 1990s about high expenditures and high tuition costs and about how much students were really learning—essentially questions about value-added—controversy over faculty responsibilities immediately flared into the open. Professors were unclear and confused about why they and the institutions of higher education were being singled out, when they after all had built such a powerful industry.

5.5 Economics: queen of the sciences

At least part of the discontent with higher education involves the ways the academic disciplines evolved by divorcing themselves from the experiences and concerns of undergraduate students. Two disciplines—economics and philosophy—serve as examples.

No social science or humanities discipline achieved higher acclaim and stature than economics after World War II. Once referred to as the dismal science, economics quickly became a beacon of American higher education, simultaneously able to assert itself as a science and to claim utilitarian value. During the first decades after the war, economics laid plausible claim "to the belief that economists had learned how to manage (if not plan) an economy; that the business cycle was largely obsolete... that full employment was a possibility; economic growth could be maintained; and that the 'Keynesian revolution' had given economists the theoretical and practical tools to achieve all these goals" (Bell, 1982, p. 30). Economics' great transformation lay in the application of mathematical model building and statistical analysis to a broad range of economic problems. In David Kreps' words, "mathematical modeling, a small piece of the subject until the 1940s and 1950s, became the all-encompassing (some would say suffocating) language of the discipline" (Kreps, 1997, p. 62). Economists were able to parlay their claims of utilitarian value with methodological rigor to become the queen of the sciences.

The ability and desire of academic economists to transform economic knowledge into an analytic toolbox and harness the power of mathematical model-building was truly revolutionary, for it substantially broadened economists' ability to make their discipline a science and to understand and to resolve complex economic and social problems. Model-building transformed the ways we understand all sorts of activities and behaviors. But it also subordinated economic history, ethics and normative judgments, and the direct observation of the real and messy world to theoretical mathematical models. For undergraduate education, these developments meant that the study of economics was, on the one hand, attractive because of its potential utility, and on the other, focused on exposure to analytic tools and model-building, which in many cases was more about technical skills than substantive economic issues. Economics for undergraduates became a version of the requirements of first year graduate students. The undergraduate's responsibility was *preparing* to do economics, learning the analytic toolbox rather than studying and understanding economic problems directly (Solow, 1997; Bell, 1982, pp. 23–30, 46–52).

The discipline of economics thus successfully defined itself in the postwar period as a field of study under little obligation to engage in conversations with undergraduate students about economic institutions or about the economic issues that concerned students. The economic literacy necessary for an educated citizenry was not the responsibility of the academic discipline of economics. Undergraduates were required less to study such topics as international trade, labor markets, the historical development of economic conditions, or the relationship between politics and economics than they were to understand the language of mathematical modeling and the use of statistical techniques.

These conditions were not uniform. The day-to-day teaching in college and university classrooms, the need to mount a full range of courses to satisfy teaching responsibilities and, not so coincidentally, to justify the appointment of more economics professors, and the academic limitations of students meant that the exposure to the methodological toolbox was not the only agenda. Economists at liberal arts colleges occasionally found themselves at odds with the emphasis on pre-graduate training within the undergraduate curriculum, since the teaching tradition at their colleges required a more comprehensive approach (Barber, 1997). Nonetheless, the heart of the discipline, the path by which economics gained promotion and prestige, lay in an approach which was resistant and even hostile to what undergraduates expected economics would be about. Little wonder then that when given the opportunity, undergraduates flocked to economics-like courses in other disciplines and interdisciplinary programs, in business schools, and in other professional schools. Indeed, it is plausible to argue that for undergraduates the most interesting economics was being taught outside economics departments.

There are a number of caveats with which one could counter my argument about the absence of conversation between the discipline of economics and undergraduates. One, commonly proffered by economists, focuses on the students and other faculty rather than on the discipline's development; the decline in academic skills among undergraduates and their disinclination to take academic work seriously after the 1960s made it difficult for students to learn the necessary tools to study economics. Often implicit in this view is that there was a decline in standards among the other academic disciplines and that the growth of economics courses for non-economists in professional schools and in other departments further lessened the enthusiasm of undergraduates for serious learning. These arguments may have some measure of truth, but they are partial at best and tend to deny that economists themselves played a role in the process.

A second caveat suggests that my description of an absence of conversation is romantic in its implied view that there ever was a conversation between economists and undergraduates prior to the dominance of mathematical modeling, and that it neglects the substantial widening of the field of economics since the 1970s. The former is probably correct and I do not mean to portray an idealized notion of economics professors in conversation with their students before the 1950s. We know enough about the evolution of the disciplines and student cultures historically to disavow a golden age of universally curious and academically committed undergraduate learners (Horowitz, 1987). But I do think that the idea of conversation has to be understood within the context of the enormous growth in stature of economics and what I believe was a genuine thirst for knowledge about economic issues among students. The case is about opportunities to improve learning foregone.

Economics did broaden its methodological focus and substantive concerns in the decades after 1970. The initial impact of mathematical modeling between 1950 and the mid-1970s had been the elimination or narrowing of the range of topics addressed in teaching and research (Kreps, 1997, pp. 65–74). That reduction shifted, in part under the pressure of the 1960s to treat non-rational behaviors, uncertain goals, and disequilibrium with the same regard as the trinity of assumptions about rationality, goal orientation, and systemic equilibrium that had dominated the previous twenty years and, in part, by the growth of "professional school" economists who focused on what they considered real world problems.

A concrete example involving the concept of educational choice might be helpful in clarifying the argument. Econometric models stress the common and shared knowledge held by decision-makers, the application of rational self-interest to decision-making, purposeful action to pursue well-defined goals and a resulting equilibrium as educational providers and educational seekers adjust to one another. This model of rational decision-making with equally available information and clarity of purpose fails in the reality that when parents and their children make educational choice decisions, they rarely have the same knowledge as everyone else, often face or have racial and religious preferences and prejudices, may be poor or wealthy, decide under various kinds of peer and familial pressures, as well as sibling rivalries, and so forth. These can be put into econometric models, but they can also be examined in ways that invite conversation about the messiness of choices about education. Students are more than able to recognize this messiness, for they encounter it in myriad ways. The more the messiness is acknowledged, the more "real" the discussion to students, who observe and experience unpredictability and irrationality all around them. However, the messier the analysis is to the economist, the more unsatisfying the approach. That, I think, separates undergraduates who are willing and may even delight in messiness from the academician's desire for methodological tidiness.

The development of economics as a discipline is suggestive of how disciplines within the academy could become methodologically more sophisticated, more precise, and grow in stature and at the same time become less and less available to students. That is not, of course, a remarkable insight. More revealing, as occurs with the absence of concern about what students are actually learning, is that there is little to prevent and little protest against the widening gap between the faculty in the discipline and the undergraduate students who are ostensibly the faculty's responsibility. Had it occurred simply in economics, such developments would have mattered little. But they occurred in other disciplines with much the same impact: as a discipline became more technical in its methodology, it lost its connection to undergraduate students. The end result was the creation of a powerful discipline-based academic organizational structure ostensibly designed to expand student learning but which failed to engender a conversation between faculty and undergraduate students on the serious issues that bound them as citizens.

5.6 Philosophy: the analytic (non) conversation

The discipline of philosophy took a path quite similar to economics, but it did so with even more devastating consequences for the conversation between itself and undergraduates.

From outside the discipline, it appeared that philosophy was poised for a substantial burst of enthusiasm and interest among students as World War II ended. Such issues as the nature of evil, social purposes, civic responsibility, and the role of the individual and the state—all of which had historically fallen within the domain of philosophy—looked ready to find a substantial student audience. This did not happen. Instead, philosophy opted for a narrowing of subject matter and methodological purity designed to separate itself from other, less rigorous disciplines and from philosophy's own history. The dominance of analytic philosophy was first and foremost a triumph of methodology with its stress on precision and clarity, on tidiness in observing, understanding, and explaining the scientific enterprise and the meaning of language. Its model was scientific precision and mathematical logic and it depended heavily on the "formal language of logical calculi," a language "that combined clear structures of logic, mathematics, and the empirical sciences" (Nehamas, 1997, pp. 212–214).

As had occurred with economics, the outcome built upon prewar developments, but it was not inevitable. In the half-century before the war, philosophers engaged in a ferocious debate over how to respond to the growing authority of science and the trends toward specialization and professionalization within the academy. The struggle, as Daniel Wilson notes, "set the stage for the rise of technical, professional philosophy, later embodied in logical positivism and analytic philosophy" and in the process, philosophers "unintentionally created the basis for philosophy's growing marginalization in 20th-century American culture, as the community of philosophic discourse contracted to a relatively small professional circle" (Wilson, 1990, pp. 1–2).

That outcome appeared self-evident in the years following the war, but the prior struggle had been a genuine one and the minority view kept latent its questions about community and civics that connected John Dewey and other pragmatists to the social concerns of the late 20th century. Yet the victors were clear: logical positivism and analytic and linguistic philosophy gave "substantive coherence" to the discipline, providing it with legitimate questions and methodologies. This approach to philosophy was self-conscious in rejecting the primacy of values, emotions, and normative judgments. Nor were philosophers to think of themselves as part of the same enterprise as historians and literary scholars, scholars with whom they had once been linked. Rather, philosophers in postwar America came to think of themselves "as participants in the enterprise of science" (Nehamas, 1997, p. 212).

There is a lot to be said for this emphasis on the precise, the logical, and the verifiable for it brought to the unfocused, the vague, and the irrational, ways of thinking that potentially allowed for the clarification and resolution of differences. But, as with mathematical model-building among economists, analytic philosophy had a way of driving alternative methodologies to the side and seeking to deny the messiness of ordinary life. In doing so, the discipline of philosophy curbed its capacity to speak with wider audiences and, in the context of higher education, its conversation with undergraduates. Academic philosophy retreated from the public domain; it observed the world but refused to engage in it. The irony of this was patent: philosophy had the potential to (and often did) address issues of interest to diverse audiences, but it did so in extremely technical terms that excluded rather than invited participation. Analytic philosophers themselves showed little inclination to open the wider conversation. As Stanley Clavell put it in 1964, "For any of the philosophers who could be called analytical, popular discussion would be irrelevant... for the analyst, philosophy has become a profession, its problems technical; a non-professional audience is of no more relevance to him than it is to the scientist" (quoted in *Daedalus*, Winter, 1997, p. 224).

In the decades after 1970, philosophy broadened both the issues it addressed and its methodological approaches, in ways that parallel economics. To a substantial degree, Thomas Kuhn's *The Structure of Scientific Revolutions* (1963) initiated the process of rethinking philosophy by reintroducing history into its daily work. A turning point came with the publication of John Rawls' *A Theory of Justice* (1970), which had an impact across the social sciences and humanities, with a subsequent expression of interest by philosophers in issues of public policy, civic and ethical judgments, and feminist ideologies, and with the resurgence of John Dewey and Deweyean concerns with public life and problem solving. These developments have affected the teaching of philosophy within philosophy departments, but, as has also been the case with economics, the greatest influences have been felt in the teaching of applied philosophy in other arts and sciences departments and in medical, business, education, and law schools where ethical issues and European continental philosophers like Habermas, Foucault, and Derrida have found homes (Nehamas, 1997, pp. 217–218).

For all their substantial differences, then, philosophy and economics have traveled parallel paths. The promise of discourse between the growing numbers and diversity of undergraduates and the two disciplines was short-circuited and left unfulfilled as the disciplines focused on methodologies that stressed mathematical models and mathematics-like logic showing little inclination to take into account the messy world that students experienced and the questions they posed about their lives and society. About the two disciplines, historian Carl Schorske writes, "The intellectual quest for scientific objectivity and the professional advantages of a value-free neutrality reinforced each other in the establishment of a new methodological consensus as the basis of the discipline [of economics]... the analytic philosophers purged or marginalized traditional areas of concern where values and feelings played a decisive role. Ethics, aesthetics, metaphysics, and politics were all for a time equally excluded as the source of pseudo-problems that could not be formulated or addressed with the rigorous canons of epistemological reliability by and out of science" (Schorske, 1997, pp. 296–299).

Recently efforts to broaden the conversation across disciplines by expanding topics and acknowledging alternative forms of knowledge and ways of knowing have occurred, but these have affected teaching and learning more outside philosophy and economics departments than within them. For the most part the failure of conversation between the two disciplines and undergraduates has been viewed as unimportant by those within each discipline and, in any event, was often ascribed to the failure of the students. Indeed, a kind of "we are not to blame" defense has set in, claiming as Alexander Nehamas has written, that the public has "no patience for any position that is not virtually self-explanatory, refusing to take seriously any view that requires careful thought and that cannot receive practical application without serious and sometimes relatively long preparation" (Nehamas, 1997, p. 220). Such a view might make sense if university and college faculty were not so dependent upon the public and students to pay the bill.

5.7 Generating a learning conversation

A real and perhaps inevitable tension exists between questions about students' learning—how much do they know, how do they learn, how do their experiences connect (or not) to their learning, what issues might challenge their minds or transform their ways of thinking and doing—and the questions faculty ask about the academic disciplines—what is known, what are the disciplinary (or interdisciplinary) questions, how should the discipline generate its questions, what are its methodologies. The different questions point in different directions. Pursuing one set rather than the other leads to quite a different understanding of what is important in the learning process.

Many professors weigh these differences seriously and, at their best, they synthesize the varied strands into a creative tension. But higher education as an entity, colleges and universities as institutions, and academic departments, including many interdisciplinary programs as collections of discipline-trained professors, have not historically made the relationship between the questions posed by how students learn and the questions posed by the disciplines as a center of attention. Professors tend to think about transferring knowledge based on the kinds of questions they might ask as disciplinary scholars. Students, in contrast, tend to think of knowledge that helps them understand and act in the world around them. Even in the best of circumstances this makes it difficult and, too often, seemingly impossible to have a sustained conversation about learning between professors and students. The absence of such a conversation has made the academy itself vulnerable, for too few students believe that the faculty or academic learning is the soul of higher education.

Do not misunderstand me. The evolution of the disciplines brought tremendous advances to our understanding of the world, substantively and methodologically. The disciplines have shown us that there are rigorous ways to ask questions, probe for answers, and summarize findings. In a relativistic world, they suggest that anyone's opinion is not as correct as anyone else's. The most important lesson we teach undergraduates is that some ways of analysis more effectively comprehend the universe than others. And, as research itself has become more interdisciplinary, so too has teaching. That said, the evolution of the academic disciplines has tended toward a rather narrow definition of what Lindblom and Cohen (1979) call "usable knowledge." The language and methods with which the disciplines work make it difficult to appreciate that using other lenses and methods are also valid ways of knowing. The disciplines in this way have worked to exclude a broader public—in Thomas Bender's phrase, they have engaged in "academic enclosure" (Bender, 1997, p. 7)—thus denying access to their knowledge and dismissing what the public knows and experiences as not being worth very much.

This combines with the tendency of the academic disciplines to misunderstand the discrepancy, in Charles Lindblom's words, "between widely accepted scientific ideals and actual feasible practice, a discrepancy that was not faced and intelligently dealt with but rather swept under the rug" (Lindblom, 1997, p. 233). Lindblom is referring specifically to the tensions within political science in the 1940s and 1950s between developing a science of political analysis and matching that to actual real world accomplishments. Similarly, Rogers Smith (1997) has argued that political science has historically wanted to be a pure science and contribute to buttressing democracy without recognizing that the desire has led to ideological blinders and has been impossible to accomplish in any event. Although their disciplinary reference point is political science, Lindblom's and Smith's arguments are applicable more generally. The academic disciplines sought scientific and methodological purity while neglecting to understand that subject matter itself became constricted and that ethical neutrality brings its own ideological baggage (Schorske, 1997).

The irony is hard to overstate; higher education entered the last half of the 20th century with an optimism never before seen in its history. An important and critical premise was that it could engage in the education of large numbers of people. And yet, even as students flocked to universities and colleges in droves, as governments expended vast sums in its support, and as local communities battled for the establishment of new campuses, scholars defined their fields in ways that made it difficult for people to understand them and in ways which proclaimed that the lack of communication did not matter. Not surprisingly, when faced with skepticism, from both outside and inside higher education, disciplinary scholars have rarely been able to convince skeptics. Even more telling, they have often viewed the skeptics and critics as irrelevant or so threatening as to require united defenses against the barbarians at the gates, leading to the view that the best defense is to convince outsiders that the subject matter was too complex for them to understand and they should, in effect, leave it alone.

Some of this has shifted. It was impossible for higher education to ignore the civil rights movement and racial conflict, the discovery of poverty and inequality, the protests over Vietnam, and the counterculture, especially when students were bringing the issues onto campuses and extending them to include the ways they were treated and taught. With the scandal of Watergate tarnishing the presidency, the shock of stagflation during the 1970s, and fears of a declining economy, the notion that scholarship and teaching should be immune from examination and revision was hard to sustain. Repeatedly, events outside higher education forced reexaminations—most recently, the worldwide financial collapse—literally demanding that colleges and universities relook at what students are actually learning. Rogers Smith's conclusion about the impact of the 1960s and 1970s on political science is broader and takes on even more power today: "In that conflict-ridden era, political science could persuasively be accused of offering models that failed to reveal and challenge unjust inequalities; to produce any behavioral laws; or to predict, explain, or provide effective social guidance concerning the startling events then occurring. And most damning of all, to an embarrassing extent, the political science literature failed even to discuss these topics" (Smith, 1997, p. 260). Such a view applies just as forcefully today to the thousands of professors and scholars in professional schools whose work failed to focus on the realities underlying economic, social, and political institutions of the early 21st century.

That said, many scholars have changed the way they go about their business, and genuine debates over knowledge, its relationship to culture and values, and its presentation to students have occurred. Perhaps the most dramatic of these is the assertion of normative claims and the explicit discussion of values in scholarship, challenging the neutrality of method that the disciplines held so dear. New topics have been invented, in part as a result of "normative claims" around inequality, justice, discrimination, the influence of gender, ethical behavior, and the study of the previously unnoticed (Schorske, 1997; Kimball, 1988). One manifestation is the willingness with which philosophers contend with one another over public issues of morality and justice, as in the 1997 brief to the Supreme Court over the right to assisted suicide (*The New York*

Review of Books, March 27, 1997). Another is the effort by educational researchers to bring their scholarly understanding of the effects of race-based financial aid to the Supreme Court (Linn and Welner, 2007). This shift to a more value-laden scholarship and to new topics that reflect normative concerns has provoked greater interest in the historical evolution of issues and of the disciplines themselves, in particular asking how things came about and why we study them in the ways we do, opening up still new approaches to fields of study (see also Walzer, 2006, Ackerman, 1991, 1998).

Real world experiences and direct observation have become fashionable. Research on "natural experiments" has grown in importance. The most remarkable methodological development is the immense popularity ethnographic research has achieved and where some of the most interesting methodological debates occur—about the immersion of the scholar in the life of the community being studied, about the relationship between those being studied and the studier, and about how replicable the findings are. These attest to a methodological shift toward qualitative research that seemed unlikely only a few decades ago. Undertaking scholarly research, quantitative and qualitative, on problems drawn from the experiences and dilemmas that people and institutions face has also increased the emphasis on the interaction between actors and structure, making indeterminacy and uncertainty a more prevalent conclusion than previously thought appropriate, wise, or scholarly (Lindblom, 1990). Disciplinary boundaries for researchers have blurred and many scholarly questions are generated by the dilemmas that people and institutions face, leading researchers to pursue whatever disciplinary approaches seem useful. Often this has had teaching consequences as more faculty than ever before teach in explicitly interdisciplinary undergraduate programs. More faculty who were trained within a discipline are thus doing research and teaching across disciplines; more undergraduates are enrolling in interdisciplinary majors; and more colleges and universities are establishing interdisciplinary teaching and research programs.

The growth of interdisciplinary research and teaching leaves higher education in an awkward organizational dilemma. Large numbers of faculty and students are engaged in interdisciplinary studies, but discipline-based departments remain the dominant organizational basis for decision-making, with the departments often acting as if each discipline was an isolated and autonomous entity. With reference to literary studies and English departments, Catherine Gallagher writes: "[We] have applied ourselves to the building of interdepartmental, rather than departmental, institutions: humanities institutes, interdisciplinary journals, women's studies programs, ethnic studies programs, film studies, team-teaching programs, and the like. While we attended to these institutional tasks, we avoided translating our ideas into coherent graduate programs... This fact may indicate that we are in the midst of an enormous institutional shift away from the traditional departments even though we continue to locate our professional training inside those [departmental] structures" (Gallagher, 1997, p. 152). That graduate doctoral programs have been so slow to acknowledge these shifts is especially disturbing since the shift toward interdisciplinary is so congruent with how many researchers actually go about their business.[3]

The rise of the professional schools and professional programs to prominence and the consequent diminution of the arts and sciences—phenomena that evolved rapidly in the 1990s under pressure to produce more "real world" and vocationally oriented programs—suggests that the traditional arts and sciences disciplines have had a difficult time engaging students in conversations about their work. There has also been a growth in orientation toward theoretical concerns, with contradictory results. Current theories almost always bring issues of race, gender, social class, ethnicity, and culture into the classroom. They tend to emphasize the historical moment, power and authority, the interaction between actors and structure, and the relative nature of values. These theoretical interests have thus had the effect of making scholarly questions seem both immediate and controversial, a scholar's dream and a student's delight. And yet the fascination with theory has many of the same ingredients as the economist's mathematical model-building and the philosopher's insistence that only logical analysis matters: it communicates a view

---

[3] On calls for graduate research training based on interdisciplinarity and real world concerns, see Yehuda Elkana (2005).

that only those who understand the theory and the language, who have, in effect, the right theoretical toolbox, can engage in the debate.

The developments described above have created tremendous uncertainty in scholarship and in teaching. What is the core of each discipline? Should there be a core? What do students need to know? Not all the disciplines have been equally affected by the debates. English departments are engulfed by them. History departments have diversified their understanding of what students need to know without necessarily tearing themselves apart. Economics and philosophy departments have often stood their ground, although the financial crisis that began toward the end of the first decade of the 21st century may have changed that. Certainly economists and philosophers outside of economics and philosophy departments have been active in taking up new methods and topics. Yet for all the differences among the disciplines, questions in higher education about what is taught, what should be taught, and how much is being learned have started to have influence. Often initiated by external agencies expressing critical doubt about the amount and quality of learning occurring among undergraduates, sometimes taking shape as arguments over political values or between new and old scholars, debates about the quality of what college students are learning have moved to the fore. For some within higher education, the debates are treated with scorn as an intrusion into their academic freedom to teach what and how they wish. Among others a kind of mournfulness appears, as if of an orderly world of the past has been shattered, a time when history, not women's history or African-American history, was taught and learned. But sometimes there is enthusiasm about addressing questions about teaching and learning, an enthusiasm generated by the possibilities of change.

Clearly, questions about the disciplines and their relationship to undergraduate learning are not easily answered. Students now have few required courses and lots of choices and the size of the curriculum remains unwieldy, testimony that faculty specialization remains dominant. It is almost impossible to tell the difference between elementary and advanced courses, except perhaps by the numbers of students enrolled in them. While it is fashionable to argue that the dismantling of a once orderly curriculum was due to the failure of nerve and the collapse of faculty authority in the face of external conditions, the curriculum disorder of the last decades is part of a disciplinary revision that began at least in the 19th century and was rooted in the dismantling of what had once been the core of each discipline. The canon may have been challenged from without higher education, but its breaking occurred from within as discipline-trained faculty looked for new problems and alternative ways to resolve them.

One should not underestimate the complexity of generating a conversation about the disciplines and their relationship to student learning. It is not easy to determine what really matters within a discipline when almost anything can be studied and a variety of methodologies are appropriate to their study. We know incredibly little about the relationship of knowledge to how students learn. Nor is it easy even to hold on to the notion that any discipline is a unique entity when so many of the same or similar issues are studied in multiple disciplines and in similar ways, whatever the professional training of the scholar. Add to these genuinely complex dilemmas the tendencies to view all potential changes through their marketability—whether they can be sold to students and funders—to phrase them in politically-charged terms or as a cover for fiscal cutbacks and the enormity of the problems are apparent.

What we do know is that students are badly under-learning and that colleges and universities do not seem capable or even willing to reverse the situation. As Derek Bok (2007) persuasively argues, many students show little improvement in writing, moral reasoning, critical thinking, and quantitative skills. Most students do not learn a foreign language, seem to develop few new cultural and aesthetic interests, and do not learn what might be considered necessary skills to participate as informed and active citizens in a democracy. This would seem to achieve the level of scandal, but almost no attention seems to be paid to this evidence by professors when they teach or discuss teaching, the latter an all too infrequent occurrence.

In fact, when looked upon from the perspective of undergraduate students, the current situation raises marvelous opportunities, for it suggests ways of looking at scholarly dilemmas that can and ought to be appealing to students, especially as the undergraduate student population itself now runs the age and experiential gamut. The possibilities of a genuine and vigorous conversation occurring between students and faculty, however, will require both a commitment on the part of the faculty to that end and a willingness to acknowledge that conversation between students and the disciplines requires a shared sense of participation and worth. And that is not easy to come by.

CHAPTER 6

A revolution in teaching and learning?*

Has a lot of rhetoric been expended on a potential revolution in teaching and learning? Yes. Have public policies emerged to require or invite improved student learning? Yes. Are numerous teaching innovations being undertaken? Some. What initiated and sustains these activities? Probably external pressures and a few people in higher education devoted to the improvement of teaching. With all this activity, why should we be so agnostic about a teaching and learning revolution? Because there are few serious incentives to improve the quality of learning and because improving the quality of learning is exceedingly difficult. There are no silver bullets!

Let's face it, there is no large-scale, serious movement to improve the quality of teaching in higher education. The claims that new technology is dramatically altering the way students learn and the ways professors teach are overstated, a cross between naïve and self-serving. If you believe them, there are a lot of other things I would like to sell you. There are, nonetheless, tremendous concerns about the quality of what students are learning, the 'value-added' by colleges or universities to what students already know. With conflicts erupting over how high tuition should be in the context of universities and colleges needing more money and students (and their families) angry at costs, issues of value-added and knowledge gained are on the table. Something is happening; we just do not know exactly what the something is.

Rumblings about the quality of teaching and learning began as a sidebar to the economic difficulties and caustic criticisms of higher education during the 1980s. Critics saw higher education as a poorly run industry, fiscally irresponsible and managerially inefficient, and they focused on organizational restructuring and ways to constrain expenses. In the jargon of the day, well-run organizations require efficient structures, strong leadership, and cost containment. Teach-

---

* A prior version was co-authored with Ursula Wagener and Nichole Shumanis.

ing and learning should also be measured along these lines, and when the critics looked, they discovered that college students learned too little, that professors taught very few hours per week, that students were leaving college before completing their degrees, and even when they did graduate, they were ill-equipped for the labor market.

The worries about teaching and learning in the early 1980s began as afterthoughts, which grew as complaints about higher education increased. Public officials picked them up and called upon professors to teach more often and more efficiently. Officials suggested that the public had a right to see evidence that students were learning and that public accountability included educational outcomes, as well as the standard reports to accrediting agencies and to auditing and accounting firms. On campuses, conversations turned to teaching and curricular innovations. Some schools tampered with their general education offerings, revising required and elective courses; many increased the number of course offerings and developed interdisciplinary majors as ways to make learning more inviting and attractive. Greater expenditures on technology to support teaching and learning occurred. A few schools, especially in the health professions, introduced competency-based learning to test how competent students were at using their knowledge. Teaching and writing centers were established, designed to help professors and graduate students become better teachers and aid students in preparing papers. Learning communities started to become popular, especially at residential schools where faculty and students could spend more time together, but also within a few community colleges. These efforts were attempts to rebalance the conversation about what matters in higher education by adding teaching and learning to the organizational restructuring, managerial changes, and cost-cutting that was coming to dominate reform. As a consequence, how professors taught and how much students learned became part of the public dialogue over higher education.

National reports by higher education organizations were one forum for stimulating interest in teaching and learning, and criticizing curricular content, teaching practices, learning outcomes, and insufficient student involvement in their learning. The rhetoric was lofty—"value-added," "collaborative and cooperative learning," "classroom assessment," and "teaching as scholarship." Studies of the brain helped educators to better understand cognitive processes. For one of the first times in American higher education history, attention focused not only on "what is taught," but "how it is taught," "what students learn, "and "how they learn it." Given the heightened attention to organizational change, the national conversation about teaching and learning that ensued raised questions about the mechanisms of change. Given the organization of higher education, how could reforms be implemented?

Many of the initial answers came from outside higher education: change had to be imposed by public bodies through a punishment-and-reward system activated through the assessment of learning outcomes. From within higher education the answer was quite different: professorial participation in shaping and implementing curricular and pedagogical change depended upon faculty buy-in. Faculty as a collective—as opposed to individual faculty members—had to be persuaded to take teaching and student learning seriously. To bring about this change, higher education's value and reward system would need modifications, including the elevation of teaching's status and a new understanding of teaching as a researchable, valued, and rewarded scholarly activity. This violated the prevailing norms that scholarship was more highly valued than teaching and that teaching was an individual faculty member's responsibility protected by academic freedom. Public demands for accountability had to be balanced, if not held in abeyance, by the sanctity of higher education's autonomy.

These conflicting presumptions—the public's demand for documented measures of accountability versus higher education's belief that its vitality depended upon maintaining its autonomy—shaped and constrained the teaching and learning revolution. Within those constraints, some within higher education engaged (and continue to engage) in vigorous efforts to encourage professors to take learning seriously, even as resistance to change remains high. The task was made even more difficult, because how to produce good learning is itself highly complex; even with the best of intentions, outcomes are always uncertain.

6.1 American education at risk

The teaching and learning reform movement took shape in the 1980s as the U.S. economy stumbled and a wave of criticism overtook elementary and secondary education. The triggering event was the Reagan administration's National Commission on Excellence in Education, *A Nation at Risk* (1983). In bold and frightening language, the Commission charged Americans with committing economic and national security suicide by failing to uphold academic standards in their schools. The curriculum, the Commission believed, had been watered down—"dumbed down" was the commonly used phrase—teachers were ill-trained, and money was being spent wastefully. Students knew little mathematics or science, read poorly, and wrote even worse. It was long past the time when public officials could ignore the nation's educational deficiencies.

A Nation at Risk initiated a national catharsis. State after state in the 1980s and early 1990s passed legislation increasing the requirements for high school graduation and demanding statewide standardized testing. The Reagan and Bush administrations of the 1980s and early 1990s, hardly proponents of increased federal intervention, introduced a national report card on how students were doing based on a series of standardized tests taken by elementary and high school students, while simultaneously opening debate about the creation of national academic achievement standards. States quickly joined in, legislating more rigorous high school graduation requirements, standardized learning assessment, and establishing minimum learning standards review committees in a variety of subjects. Mandates for more comprehensive teacher assessment led to the creation of new organizations or invigorated interest from existing organizations to hold teachers to higher academic standards. Educational outcomes—what students actually knew—took on greater importance, with the debate centering on how to determine what they should know and how to implement measures to make more learning happen. The movement to improve the quality of elementary and secondary learning was given still further impetus when the results of international achievement tests showed American students to be behind their counterparts around the world (Elmore and Fuhrman, 1990).

By the early 1990s, the charges that America's public schools were malfunctioning had stimulated a host of efforts, some contradictory, to improve the quality of teaching and learning. The tension between accountability measures, largely driven by those outside the educational system, and the attempts within schools to reconceptualize the environments for students' learning—by, for example, introducing smaller classes—was often palpable. Demands for higher academic standards and more standardized testing of outcomes, a more rigorous curriculum, better teacher training, portfolios that assessed student learning, the reorganization of school districts and individual schools into smaller entities, the creation of charter schools, greater parental choice, and increased parental involvement in their children's education, all competed with one another. At the same time, a new mantra of learning, based in part upon research into how children learn, told educators to make schools more "learner-centered." Translated, this seemed to mean some combination of holding all students to higher academic standards, emphasizing active learning and student engagement, making schoolwork relevant to students, and individualizing instruction.

Inescapably, criticisms of elementary and secondary schooling spilled over into higher education. One source came from the corporate sector. During the early 1980s, with a national economy in the doldrums and seemingly being overwhelmed by Asia's boom, corporate leaders undertook massive restructuring of their operations. They quickly conceived of higher education's problems in the same terms, as ones of organizational inefficiencies, weak governance and decision-making structures, poor leadership, and excessive costs of operation artificially hidden by rapidly rising tuition charges. Politicians weighed in, painting higher education with the same "tax and spend" brush that so successfully spearheaded Republican political triumphs. Public colleges and universities were like other public agencies—overly subsidized and protected by government from the rigors of marketplace competition. Professors became another version of federal bureaucrats, in the language of the day, simply putting in their time without being held to clear measures of accountability. Angrily, critics charged that professors taught too few students for too few hours with too little interest. Academic leaders were denounced as weak and obstructionist, unwilling or unable to make forceful decisions in a timely fashion. As Harvard's president, Derek Bok, noted in the mid-1980s, "Governors and other public figures are openly wondering just what results are being obtained in exchange for the billions spent on higher education" (Bok, 1986).

The attacks were vitriolic, the kind of anger that comes from trust betrayed. The higher education system that had grown so fast and become so powerful had badly stumbled and was in urgent need of repair. In what became the standard litany of the 1980s, Chester Finn, Jr., a former official in the U.S. Department of Education, issued an indictment of colleges and universities for admitting unqualified students, coddling them, and resisting genuine assessments of student learning. Explicitly tying his critique to the emergent criticism of America's public schools, Finn charged that "American colleges and universities have thus far largely escaped the intense scrutiny to which our elementary and secondary schools have been subjected. This reprieve should not, however, be taken as proof that higher education has somehow eluded the qualitative decay that has weakened the schools" (Finn, 1984).

Voices from corporate America reinforced these views. With corporate leaders assuming greater influence on state boards of higher education and boards of trustees, attention centered on organizational and economic failings, with business leaders faulting colleges and universities for not adopting the principles of corporate America—cutting costs, re-engineering and restructuring business operations, and demanding more efficient and more productive workers—and for not having a genuine 'bottom line.' In contrast to the world of business, colleges and universities lacked serious mechanisms of accountability. Indeed, in order to counter this notion that higher education lacked accountability, higher education began to refer to student learning as its bottom line. Public officials quickly acknowledged that this might be the case, and then turned back to higher education to demand proof that it was in fact producing results. As Governor John Ashcroft of Missouri, chair of the National Governors' Association Task Force on College Quality, wrote, "The public has the right to know what it is getting for its expenditure of tax resources; the public has a right to know and understand the quality of undergraduate education that young people receive from publicly funded colleges and universities. They have a right to know that their resources are being wisely invested and committed" (National Governors' Association, 1986).

6.2 Learning, assessment, and accountability

The view that higher education was in deep need of reform found expression in a host of national reports through the 1980s, from the National Institute of Education (1984), the National Endowment for the Humanities (Bennett, 1984), the Association of American Colleges (1985), and the Carnegie Foundation for the Advancement of Teaching (Newman, 1985). Perhaps the report with the greatest public policy impact, the National Governors' Association's *Time for Results* appeared in 1986. Chaired by three of the country's most prominent governors—Lamar Alexander of Tennessee, future president Bill Clinton of Arkansas, and Thomas Kean of New Jersey—*Time for Results* painted a broad canvas of what was needed for states to improve the condition of elementary, secondary, and collegiate education. To the governors the need for reform was self-evident: economic productivity required a better-educated workforce.

The Governors' Association Task Force on College Quality concentrated on learning, or more accurately, as the task force's chair wrote, on the lack of "a systematic way to demonstrate whether student learning is taking place." For the governors, the central learning issue was assessment: "The Task Force on College Quality decided to focus on how colleges and universities can *demonstrate* that student learning is occurring. In addition to investigating how colleges and universities can assess student learning, the task force also studied data on how student outcomes can be used to assess the effectiveness of academic programs, curriculums, and institutions" (National Governors' Association, 1986, pp. 20–21, 154–165).

The report highlighted the dominant theme in the public's perception of what was needed to improve higher education—stronger measures of accountability. Public assessment of student learning was especially important because it would hold colleges and universities accountable in their primary business, teaching and learning. Assessment of student learning was a way to account for the large expenditures of public funds given to higher education, a way to justify the powerful influence colleges and universities had in awarding status to individuals, and, for some, a way to reverse the public's loss of confidence in higher education. In this sense, the assessment of learning paralleled the bottom line in business, a way to account for the investments and a mechanism to improve return on investment.

Assessment as public policy grew swiftly. Almost no state in the early 1980s required institutions of higher education to assess their students' learning beyond the usual fare of course examinations and papers. By the end of the decade more than 40 states had taken action designed to get public universities and colleges to assess learning outcomes, and all six regional accrediting associations included outcomes assessment in their criteria for accreditation of both public and private institutions. Assessment of student learning, Patricia Hutchings and Theodore Marchese of the American Association of Higher Education concluded in 1990, was becoming "a condition of doing business" (Hutchings and Marchese, 1990).

Actual state assessment polices varied, from those that mandated statewide testing of students (e.g., Florida) to those that sought to encourage institutional reporting on a variety of indicators of effectiveness as part of a general review process (Aper and Hinkle, 1991). Most states opted to require institutions to develop their own local assessment procedures consistent with their missions and student consumers. Such an approach was intended to acknowledge institutional autonomy and to allay schools' fears of inter-institutional comparisons. At the same time, set-aside funds were made available to institutions in the form of grant-like incentive pools to encourage instructional innovation consistent with assessment.

At the federal level, the Fund for the Improvement of Post-secondary Education (FIPSE), which had historically been at the center of efforts at innovation, turned its support to the development of campus assessment programs. The National Association of State Universities and Land-Grant Colleges (NASULGC) responded to the continued expansion of state assessment efforts by promulgating guiding principles regarding assessment policies, including focusing on the effectiveness of academic programs and the improvement of student learning and performance, calling upon states to use incentives rather than regulations or penalties, and to develop such incentives collaboratively with faculty.

Fairly early on then, the broad shape of the assessment movement was set. States pressed colleges and universities to take the assessment of learning seriously and to use the outcomes data to reshape their curriculum and to alter teaching in order to improve what and how much students learned. Higher education organizations, like NASULGC, urged states to provide incentives for institutions to use learning assessment as a mechanism of change and urged campuses to "own" assessment as a way to improve academic programs and increase student learning—and not incidentally, to protect institutional autonomy. On one level, then, Hutchings and Marchese were right: by the 1990s the assessment movement was making major inroads into higher education and was playing an important role in prodding colleges and universities to talk about student learning.

However, that was only part of the story. Faculty tended to view assessment as externally imposed and having little to do with their business of research and teaching, as well as being sensitive to the political and economic uses that state-imposed assessments could be put. Assessment also seemed yet another reporting requirement in a growing list of such requirements, and faculty responded negatively to the intrusiveness of the demands. With few incentives to cooperate, at least as perceived by faculty, professors showed little enthusiasm for being held responsible for student learning. The traditional norm was that professors brought knowledge to the classroom and taught it; college students chose to learn it or not. Postsecondary education, after all, was optional, not compelled. That norm among faculty was not easily overturned (Ewell, 1999; Banta and Associates, 1993).

Multiple problems existed. One involved the conflicting messages, those being sent by the externally driven assessment movement and those being received by institutions. Because the assessment movement emerged out of the cascade of criticism about higher education, it became inseparable from efforts to hold colleges and universities accountable and often seemed more about accountability and power than about improving the quality of learning.

Even those faculty genuinely interested in improving student learn-ing found themselves fighting against a perception that doing so would be to capitulate to the bullying tactics that threatened higher education's autonomy. Public bodies found the organizational com-plexities of colleges and universities confusing and frustrating. Meanwhile political and corporate leaders had little patience for inaction. Most higher education institutions had little experience in collective decision-making and even less in having to make and implement decisions quickly. Despite the rhetoric of shared gover-nance and faculty responsibility for an institution's success, most higher education institutions were collections of schools and depart-ments that functioned fairly autonomously from one another, often viewing each other as involved in a zero sum gain, where one department's gains were perceived as losses elsewhere. With the bulk of the faculty holding tenure, there existed few mechanisms to require change. The traditional pattern of leaving decisions about teaching and curriculum to individual faculty members and depart-ments remained in place. It was hard to hold a meaningful conver-sation or to agree on new rules of the game in such circumstances.

There were also serious and almost totally unaddressed ques-tions about the relationships between assessments of learning and changes in academic programs and teaching. What did it mean to instructors when they were told that their students were not per-forming well on writing or historical knowledge? There were the dilemmas of measurement itself as well. Faculty rightly asked such questions as: "What do we want to know?" "Why do we want to know it?" "How should we measure it?" "What will we do with the answers?" Such questions were both defensive reactions to external pressures—ways of setting up shields until the political clamor died down—and genuine attempts to comprehend what was worth doing and how.

By the end of the 1990s, it had become obvious that state-man-dated assessments had not altered undergraduate education; public officials consequently lost patience with the slow pace of change and the occasional outright resistance of some (often prominent) institutions to the assessment agenda (Ewell, 1999). They became frustrated with the difficulties in getting clear measures of what students were learning and the difficulties in comparing data across institutions when assessment measures were being created institution by institution, thus making it exceedingly difficult to use the information to make budgetary and funding allocation decisions. With change barely noticeable, state legislatures and state boards of higher education shifted from the view that colleges and universities should set the terms of campus-based assessments, thereby giving substantial freedom to institutions and complicating inter-institutional comparisons, and started to demand more standardized and more easily measured indicators of performance: enrollment and graduation rates; degree completion and time to degree; persistence and retention rates; remediation activities and indicators of their effectiveness; transfer rates to and from two- and four-year institutions; pass rates on professional exams; job placement data on graduates and graduates' satisfaction with their jobs; and faculty workload and productivity in the form of student-faculty ratios and instructional contact hours (Burke and Serban, 1998a, 1998b).

The shift to performance outcomes and common indicators that could be more easily obtained, more easily quantified, and more easily compared attested to the complexities involved in measuring learning, and were simpler ways public agencies could make comparative analyses for budgetary allocations. These kinds of measurable outcomes could be viewed as alternative ways of assessing teaching and learning. Graduation rates, amounts of remediation, degree completion time, job placement, and faculty workload could serve as surrogates for direct measures of learning. And such data could be gotten from more compliant college and university administrators without excessive dependence on faculty buy-in. In short order, efforts shifted from state mandates that institutions create campus-based assessments to the creation of state-required performance-funding and performance-budgeting. The former tied state funds directly to public college and university achievement of designated indicators; the latter took a laundry list of indicators into consideration in determining higher education budgets.

The movement toward common indicators tied to institutional and system-wide performance outcomes achieved robust growth. In 1998 half the states were using some form of performance indicators in their budgetary allotments to institutions and statewide systems, including Colorado, Connecticut, Florida, Georgia, Illinois,

Indiana, Mississippi, Nebraska, North Carolina, Ohio, Oregon, Tennessee, Texas, and Washington. The Rockefeller Institute of Government projected that even more states were likely to move in that direction in the next five years (Burke and Serban, 1998[a]). Although most performance-based budgeting policies affected less than 5% of the higher education budgets—sometimes available as new money offered as incentives—the policies were explicitly aimed to get institutions to change the ways they did business. In Tennessee, the first state to implement performance-budgeting, roughly 5% of the state's budget for higher education was earmarked for incentive bonuses for institutions that met or exceeded state-determined and institutionally-defined goals, such as improved student performance on various tests and student and alumni satisfaction with their education. South Carolina's General Assembly passed a more ambitious financing system in 1996, in which the amount of money that each public college received from the state depended entirely on its progress in meeting a list of goals (Schmidt, 1996).

As the 21st century began, the assessment movement was both flourishing and in shambles. As an externally driven phenomenon, the movement had forced student learning onto higher education's agenda. A survey of chief academic officers at almost 1,400 public and private institutions showed that the overwhelming majority— between 74 percent and 96 percent depending on the measure— reported collecting student assessment data, including progress to degree, basic college readiness skills, academic intentions, and student satisfaction with their undergraduate experience. But beneath the movement's rapid implementation were some jolting revelations. Only around a third of the institutions assessed students' higher order learning skills, affective development, or professional skills. The use of alternative forms of assessment, like the much talked about portfolios, capstone projects, and observations of student performance was infrequent. "Most institutions' approaches emphasize the use of easily quantifiable indicators of student progress and pay less attention to more complex measures of student development." Most powerfully, there was little evidence that any of the institutional assessment measures were being used either to improve institutional approaches to student learning or to make budgetary allocations (National Center for Postsecondary Improvement, 1999).

The assessment movement was neither assessing learning in any direct sense nor was it connecting the findings of the assessments to faculty teaching, evaluations, or rewards. The disjunction between the assessments and faculty behavior remained substantial. To some extent, these failures derived from the externally driven nature of the assessment movement. Campus conversations often became mired down in complaints over assessment's imposition and its threats to academic integrity rather than on the ways faculty taught and students learned. In contrast to the more hierarchical governance of corporations, higher education institutions had little experience in reaching collective decisions linked to quick implementation. Faculty trained to teach their disciplines showed little interest in assessments that went beyond the norms of course examinations and papers; they rarely possessed much understanding of how to link data from assessments to the ways they taught. Institutional leaders were themselves reluctant to press for concrete linkages between assessment's findings and faculty classroom activities. Most often, they settled for the collection of data in ways that made their institution look good and help reduce political pressures. For many faculty, a heightened emphasis on teaching and learning seemed to put their commitments to research, and the status attached to research, at risk. While most academic administrators—72% in the survey cited above—reported they strongly supported student assessments, these same administrators identified only 24% of their faculty as being very supportive of student-assessment measures. Interpreting the survey, Ted Marchese, *Change's* executive editor and vice president of the American Association for Higher Education, concluded: "the assessment movement, following 15 years of imprecation and mandate, has produced widely observed rituals of compliance on campus, but these have had only minor impacts on the aims of the practice—to improve student learning and public understanding of our contributions to it. To say the least, this is a disappointment" (Marchese, 1999).

6.3 Voices of reform

The assessment movement was a high-profile public campaign to improve the quality of teaching and learning on college and university campuses. Its ambiguous results during the 1980s and 1990s attested to the difficulties of externally imposing changes on the ways institutions, and especially faculty, went about their business. From within higher education itself, however, other attempts to kindle stronger allegiances to the quality of student learning were being undertaken. In particular, a small group of individuals, in many cases linked to national higher education organizations, led a campaign to get colleges and universities to take teaching and student learning seriously. They were joined by faculty and administrators on numerous campuses pressing to reorient and invigorate their schools' commitments to teaching and learning by connecting their goals to institutional missions and academic values.

Aware of how politically difficult change would be, especially at the large research-oriented universities, the learning reformers recognized the need to play the "imperative" card, that external pressures demanded change, while being careful not to provoke further faculty backlash with heavy-handed threats. They understood that professors held fast to the norms of faculty autonomy, the right to pursue the research of their choice and to conduct their classes largely unfettered by bureaucratic constraints or oversight. The reformers appreciated that higher education's value system, even at many self-described "teaching" institutions, placed research at the top of the status hierarchy. It was thus necessary, the reformers believed, to show that teaching could be a scholarly, researchable activity. The reformers recognized that most professors knew little about alternative forms of teaching or ways of assessing their teaching, and that changes in teaching practice were time consuming. The learning reformers understood that their calls to invigorate teaching and learning challenged higher education's institutional culture.[1]

---

[1] Obviously sharp differences exist among colleges and universities in the ways they treat research and teaching. Nonetheless the ethos of research is so powerful that its spillover profoundly affects every level

The national and local conversations on the improvement of teaching and learning that emerged were both defensive and proactive, designed simultaneously to blunt the interventions of external agencies and to turn faculty attention toward teaching and learning. The reformers called upon colleges and universities to make teaching and learning legitimate subjects of research and to focus on assessment and research in the classroom. A new language about the scholarship of teaching emerged, along with recommendations to modify a rigid research-oriented promotion system for faculty. Faced with the externally driven assessment and accountability pressures, the reformers contended that highlighting the importance of teaching and learning would protect institutional autonomy from encroachment by external agencies. Acknowledging the highly competitive market for students, they understood that the failure to show substantial interest in student learning undermined an institution's attractiveness to students, with resulting fiscal consequences. Perhaps most poignantly, they valued student learning for its own sake, believing that higher education had been led astray in neglecting it. Six of these higher education reformers achieved particular prominence: Alexander Astin of the Higher Education Research Institute at UCLA; Derek Bok and Richard Light of Harvard University; Ernest Boyer of the Carnegie Foundation for the Advancement of Teaching; K. Patricia Cross of Harvard, UC-Berkeley and the American Association for Higher Education (AAHE); and Lee Shulman of Stanford University and the Carnegie Foundation for the Advancement of Teaching. They were not alone; on numerous campuses, groups of faculty and administrators engaged in battles to reshape faculty and student responsibility toward learning. But these six captured national attention; they were frequently cited and used on campuses to make the case for reform. Their stories illuminate what was happening.

---

and almost every institution, with the result that efforts to improve teaching and learning have to take the research reward system into account. Since there are very few direct challenges to the research imperative, efforts to improve the quality of learning almost always have to walk gingerly around the research question.

Learning environments: Alexander Astin

In the early and mid-1980s, Alexander Astin, director of the UCLA's Higher Education Research Institute, articulated two paths for learning reformers to follow. Having achieved national prominence for his work on student values, most notably through an annual survey of college freshmen that was administered to more than 375,000 students each year at about 700 two- and four-year colleges, Astin's first path challenged higher education's ways of measuring educational quality; his second called for a new emphasis on learning environments.

Astin began by claiming that the four traditional standards typically used to measure quality were badly flawed:
- quality as measured by *resources* (e.g., endowment, external research funding);
- quality as measured by *reputation* (e.g., faculty prestige, professional attainment of graduates);
- quality as measured by *student outcomes* (e.g., retention and graduation rates, salaries of graduates); and
- quality as measured by *curricular content.*

These measures had little to do with the actual accomplishments of colleges in teaching their students. They said nothing about results—how well a college's students learned what they were taught. A college's quality, he argued, should instead be measured by the value added to its students' learning and by the extent to which a college extended the talents of its students. If learning was to be taken seriously, higher education had to factor learning directly into assessments of institutional quality—and by extension, into an institution's prestige (Astin, 1985a, 1985b).

Astin's second path more directly attended to learning itself: campuses and classrooms had to be reorganized to engage students if they were actually to learn. Initially in articles and then more widely under the aegis of the National Institute of Education's *Involvement in Learning* (1984)—Astin was a member of the panel that drafted the report—he argued that effective learning required high expectations, student involvement in their own learning, and assessment and feedback as a means of furthering learning, themes similarly being articulated by many K-12 educational reformers. Indeed, the idea that schools of all kinds could be reorganized into more powerful learning environments was being supported by an outpouring of research on how people learn (Bransford, Brown, and Cocking, 1999). The standard methods of teaching—lecturing and discussion sections—it was clear, would not engage students. By the mid-1980s, Astin's emphasis on student academic outcomes based on assessments of "value-added" as measures of institutional quality and his belief that campuses could be reorganized to focus on learning were being picked up. In 1985, the Association of American Colleges' *Integrity in the College Curriculum* (1985) defined educational quality in terms of student learning. Beginning with "the problems"—declining SAT scores; college graduates with serious deficiencies in writing and lacking scientific and technical understanding; a curriculum without depth, breadth, or coherence; and professors who were too specialized and too concerned with research—the report advocated a college curriculum that emphasized modes of inquiry rather than a set of required courses. Colleges should emphasize "how to learn" rather than "what to learn," phrases congruent with Astin's views (Wagener, 1989).

Astin's voice sketched out two of the paths that learning reformers would and continue to travel. The first claimed that as long as measurements of institutional quality and status failed to include an institution's contribution to student learning, little incentive existed to improve teaching. It simply made no sense to think of institutional quality without thinking about the quality of learning, thereby giving shape to the Quality Assessment movement of the last few decades. The second path contended that learning could not be improved without altering campus and classroom learning environments. The typical format of professors giving information to students and the students dutifully learning it was not going to have any substantial affect on learning, even when it occurred via technology. Both of Astin's paths had to be followed. Assessments of learning had to be taken into account in reputational rankings of institutional quality and students had to be involved in their own learning if they were to learn. The paths were simultaneously clear and hard to follow.

The Harvard dynamic: Derek Bok and Richard J. Light

Derek Bok, Harvard University's president from 1971 to 1991, who served a short term as acting president in the early 2000s, was an unlikely candidate to push teaching and learning reform. But, like a number of other leaders of higher education in the 1980s, Bok was concerned with the public's anger and bewilderment about sky-rocketing tuition and the results of the billions of dollars annually spent on higher education. For higher education's private sector, pressure to reform came from parents, potential students, the media, and a heightened competitive environment, rather than from state legislators and state accountability measures. Responding to these pressures, Bok asked, "What do we really know about the value of a college education? In fact, the evidence we have is at once thin and disturbing... There is little cause for celebration in research findings indicating that the average [college] senior knows only as much as students at the 84th percentile of the freshman class; it is even more disturbing to note other findings that reveal much lower rates of progress in such important activities as critical thinking and expository writing." Adopting Astin's language of value added, and essentially accepting that powerful external pressures demanded that higher education develop a marketplace bottom-line, Bok concluded that universities and colleges had to show that they genuinely added to their students' knowledge. He urged faculty to determine common goals for undergraduate education, to connect those goals to their individual teaching, and to work to help students learn how to learn. While not giving way on the importance of research faculty at research universities, Bok exhorted the higher education community to take teaching and student learning seriously (Bok, 1986), a theme he has continued to take up (Bok, 2007).

Seeking to reshape how college students learned was not a new phenomenon for Harvard, although the voice of reform had been largely absent from national conversations about education since the 1960s. That had not always been the case. In the last decades of the 19th century, Harvard President Charles William Eliot instituted a revolution in higher education by making electives—faculty and student choice in what to teach and to learn—the centerpiece of the university's curriculum. The "house system" of the 1920s at Harvard and Yale ushered in a conception of living and learning that became a continuing motif of educational reformers. In the immediate aftermath of World War II, the Harvard faculty's *Redbook* articulated an approach to undergraduate education that emphasized general education in the interests of creating more knowledgeable and responsible citizens.

Still, Bok's entry into the national debate about teaching and learning was surprising. Even more so was his decision to ask his Harvard colleagues to examine Harvard's learning environment, an examination that Bok himself was undertaking in his annual reports on the quality of the university's various schools. To facilitate the examination, he turned to a statistics professor, Richard Light, who held appointments at both Harvard's Graduate School of Education and the Kennedy School of Government, to oversee a series of seminars with people from within and outside Harvard. Beginning in the fall of 1986, an initial group of 27 Harvard faculty and administrators convened the Harvard Assessment Seminars; over the next four years the group expanded to include more than 100 people drawn from more than two dozen colleges and universities. They sought to "encourage innovation in teaching, in curriculum, in advising, and to evaluate the effectiveness of each innovation." Bok himself expressed his commitment to the enterprise by attending the Seminars' regular monthly meetings for the first six months of their existence.

Working in small groups comprised of faculty, administrators, and students, the Seminars surveyed samples of Harvard College undergraduates and alumni and then issued a nationally disseminated report (Light, 1990). Among the findings: student learning increased when students had immediate feedback on quizzes and assignments and when they were given opportunities for revision. Students learned better in small classes, when they used study groups, and when they shared their written papers with peers ahead of class. Not surprisingly, the findings were congruent with Alexander Astin's views and the National Institute of Education's *Involvement in Education* (1984). The most often cited teaching tip derived from a suggestion of Seminar participant K. Patricia Cross, that professors should use a "one-minute paper," which asks students to respond to two questions at the end of each class: 1) What is the big point you learned in class today? and 2) What is the main unanswered question you leave class with today? Each of the questions was designed to foster student learning through active listening and to get students to think of the broad goals of the class rather than the details of any particular topic. As noted below, Cross' instant replay paper was part of her effort to channel higher education's assessment movement into classroom practice based on what faculty believed they were trying to accomplish.

The Harvard Assessment Seminars helped advance discussions of teaching and learning among Harvard's faculty, administrators, students, and alumni, while staying clear of any substantial assessment of Harvard's teaching practices or student outcome measures, ironically, two of the things Bok had found most important. The impact at Harvard itself is difficult to assess. The most concrete example of impact occurred in Harvard's Danforth Center for Teaching and Learning, which was renamed in honor of Derek Bok and shifted its traditional almost exclusive focus on graduate student teaching assistants to pay more attention to faculty teaching. Light himself has been unflagging in his commitment to improve learning on college and university campuses (Light, 2001).

The national response to the results of the Harvard Assessment Seminars was substantial and immediate—Light called it "astonishing"—for they hit the higher education community at precisely the moment when teaching and learning were becoming public issues. Light initially requested that 1,000 copies be printed, primarily for distribution within Harvard. By the late 1990s, he had received 18,000 requests for copies; the number reproduced on campuses is incalculable. Much to his surprise, Light became a national spokesperson for improved teaching and a greater focus on student learning. His advice was sound and practical: pay more attention to how your students learn, stimulate greater interaction among them, respond quickly to their work, and ask them to assess what they have learned on an ongoing basis. Although the reports shied away from confronting higher education's research-oriented reward and value system, they contained within them implicit and potentially powerful notions: universities and professors should take greater responsibility for how much their students learn and there were practical steps that would improve learning.

Derek Bok and Richard Light combined to give further legitimization to the emergent focus on teaching and learning. Bok's challenge that colleges and universities show value-added learning as an outcome of enrollment helped to push higher education toward a greater focus on outcomes, toward some notion of the business world's bottom-line. Light's proposals to modify teaching in the interests of greater student learning brought substance to what were often vague pleas to teach better. And, the implicit notion that faculty had more direct responsibility for how much their students learned held the seeds of a potential revolution.

The scholarship of teaching: Ernest L. Boyer

In the half-century after World War II, higher education's faculty reward system became dominated by the ethos of research. Institutional stature and individual professorial prestige were intimately connected to research productivity, externally funded research grants, and awards for scholarly research. So powerful was the ethos of research that many colleges and universities with self-proclaimed teaching missions substantially increased the role of research in faculty hiring and promotions until it became a given of professorial life—even as few faculty actually did very much of it. The conundrum for the teaching and learning reforms was simple to state, but exceedingly difficult to resolve. Given the enchantment with research, how could institutions and faculty be convinced to dignify teaching with the same status as research? How could higher education shift from teaching as an honored but invisible activity, to use W. Norton Grubb's phrase, to teaching that was both honored and visible (Grubb, et. al., 1999)?

The answer was actually quite simple, at least at the level of rhetoric. For Ernest Boyer, as well as for K. Patricia Cross and Lee Shulman (discussed below), higher education had to connect teaching and learning to faculty disciplinary and professional life. In particular, Boyer believed that scholarship could be redefined in such a way as to incorporate a wide variety of faculty work, including teaching. President of the Carnegie Foundation for the Advancement of Teaching between 1979 and his death in 1995, former U.S. Commissioner of Education, and former Chancellor of the State University of New York, Boyer's solution to the dilemma of how to give teaching public importance was brilliant: teaching would be recognized as a legitimate subject of research. As such, it could be subjected to the same kind of peer assessments as research. Rather than attacking higher education's preoccupation with scholarly productivity, and thus asking higher education to choose between research and teaching in a zero-sum game, Boyer called for teaching itself to become a scholarly activity.

Two reports by the Carnegie Foundation, both issued in 1987, initiated Boyer's campaign. Burton R. Clark's *The Academic Life* (1987) covered the landscape of what constituted professorial work. A well-respected sociologist whose article on the "cooling-out process" of community colleges was considered seminal by higher education scholars, Clark's book highlighted the "paradox of academic work:" most professors teach most of the time and many professors teach all of the time and do not publish scholarly studies, but teaching is neither highly valued nor highly rewarded. Rewards went for something in which only a very limited number of professors were engaged—research (Clark, 1987, p. 98). Boyer's *College: the Undergraduate Experience in America* (1987) presented the results of a three-year study of 29 colleges, highlighting a series of tensions embedded in higher education: discontinuity between colleges and high schools, student-versus-faculty expectations in the classrooms, and the pressure to publish versus teaching commitments. These tensions, Boyer believed, manifested deep confusion over institutional goals and revealed the need to establish a clear and vital collegiate mission. And that required an "integrated core... a program of general education that introduces students not only to general knowledge, but to connections across the disciplines, and in the end, to the application of knowledge to life beyond the campus" (p. 91).

Boyer's complaints and his proposed integrated core within a general education program were hardly new and his curricular prescriptions did not seem likely to elicit much comment or attention. Boyer's centrality in the emergent discussion of learning came instead from his attempt to re-situate teaching as a research activity. Highlighting Clark's finding that most professors spent most to all of their time teaching, Boyer claimed that most faculty, even those at small teaching colleges, nonetheless believed that research was more highly valued than teaching. Professors believed they worked in a system in which their primary activity—teaching—was diminished. And that problem, they and Boyer concluded, was rooted in a reward system that overemphasized research.

Boyer's answer, articulated in his most widely cited and controversial work, *Scholarship Reconsidered: Priorities of the Professoriate* (1990), broadened the definition of scholarship itself by defining in more creative ways what it meant to be a scholar. Rather than reject the value of scholarly research, a position that would have pitted him against the dominant trend of higher education, Boyer sought to convert teaching into a legitimate scholarly endeavor. He began by articulating four separate but overlapping functions of scholarship: discovery, integration, application, and teaching. He affirmed the importance of "the scholarship of discovery" (basic research) and of applied scholarship devoted to resolving social, economic, and ecological problems, the two kinds of research higher education traditionally recognized and rewarded. But Boyer went further arguing that professors should be promoted and tenured for writing textbooks, for popular writing, for consulting and technical assistance to organizations, all ways of integrating knowledge and communicating it to larger audiences than those reached by traditional scholarship. These areas were infrequently commended or even taken into account by scholarly review committees. To give teaching even more legitimacy, Boyer believed, it needed to have its own rigorous assessment process. Boyer's message was to give teaching the same weight as research by subjecting it to rigorous assessments and by allowing professors to consider the creation of curriculum and the improvement of their teaching as a scholarly activity.

Tireless in disseminating his views, it seemed as if *Scholarship Reconsidered* was placed on almost every college and university president's desk, a way of announcing to faculty and the public that "my institution" was paying attention. Professional organizations hosted sessions, often with Boyer as the keynote speaker. College and university administrators wanting to increase faculty commitments to teaching and to improve its quality began to use Boyer's work to require fuller teaching dossiers in promotion and tenure decisions. Teaching as a scholarly activity—a phrase borrowed from elementary and secondary classroom research—became a new higher education buzz word, what Lee Shulman, who replaced Boyer as head of CFAT, called the rendering of "one's own practice as the problem for investigation" (Shulman, 1999).

And yet, while it had become hard by the end of the 1990s to ignore poor teaching, especially as institutions competed for students, and while some Ph.D. programs expressed greater interest in having their graduate students become better teachers, there was an add-on quality to the new emphasis on teaching. Boyer's efforts seemed to further complicate being a professor, for one would have to be successful as a disciplinary-based researcher, as a researcher of one's own teaching, and as a teacher. Faculty promotion would require successful teaching with no diminution of research productivity and the addition of a second line of research into teaching.

Nonetheless, Boyer's proposal to give teaching greater weight by according it scholarly status received enormous rhetorical support and helped make teaching and learning a legitimate conversation on college campuses. At the end of the 1990s, his commitment to teaching as a scholarly activity received a substantial boost when the foundation he had led, in cooperation with the American Association for Higher Education, initiated major efforts to convert "rhetoric to action" (Hutchings and Shulman, 1999; Shulman, 1999). Boyer's re-conceptualization provocatively offered a way to integrate teaching with scholarship for institutions reluctant to diminish their research agendas. Politically astute in understanding higher education's ethos, he opened a door through which the learning reformers could try to walk.

Classroom assessment and classroom research:
K. Patricia Cross

Most of higher education's teaching and learning reformers were stronger on ideas and sweeping proposals than on developing concrete ways to change collegiate classrooms. Ways to implement new pedagogical strategies, deepen student learning, and be more creative in assessing learning were few and far between. The state-based assessment movement offered little help. While legislators and governors demanded greater accountability for learning, they essentially left methods to the same campuses and the professors who had, by and large, neither been invested in student learning nor been particularly creative in how to teach so that students learned more. How to conduct classrooms in which students learned had, however, begun to attract the attention of a few individuals and organizations. None was more influential than K. Patricia Cross. An initial member of Light's assessment seminars while a Senior Lecturer at the Harvard Graduate School of Education before becoming Gardner Professor of Higher Education at the University of California, Berkeley, Cross established an international reputation during the 1970s at the Educational Testing Service for her work on community colleges, adult learners, and lifelong learning (*Beyond the Open Door*, 1971; *Accent on Learning*, 1976; *Adults as Learners*, 1981). As an officer of the American Association for Higher Education and a member of its board of directors, she actively pressed student learning as higher education's primary agenda. Cross believed that teaching was a profoundly intellectual challenge, one refreshed by the opportunity to assess the impact of one's teaching on students' learning. It was thus important, if the learning reform movement was to make serious inroads into higher education's practices, to make its ideas concrete. She did that by offering advice on how to assess one's teaching and undertake classroom research to the benefit of students. Connected by her earlier work to the nation's community colleges and the realization that adult learners should be taught differently than 18 and 19-year-olds, Cross used her stature to gain access to public universities that were especially vulnerable to the existing political pressures to show improved learning. She made "how to do it" her calling card.

Cross contributed two arguments to the learning reform movement. First, she found that almost no relationship existed between research on learning and collegiate teaching practices; college teachers paid little or no attention to what their learning research colleagues discovered. Second, she concluded that student feedback and the assessment of students could be used to improve teaching and student learning, provided these were done in a timely manner. The learning research community was having so little impact on college campuses because its work failed to pay attention to the actual classroom experiences of teachers—a charge also being laid against researchers in elementary and secondary education.

Researchers on teaching and learning talked *at* rather than *with* faculty in an environment that undervalued teaching anyway. Professors were either oblivious to the research or ignored it, helping to explain why national reports were more rhetorical flights of fancy than agendas for change. Reflecting on the disconnect between learning research and teaching practice in a 1998 speech, Cross declared: "I am distressed to see researchers—the acknowledged authorities of our times—talk about learning with no reference to the experience of teachers who have spent lifetimes accumulating knowledge about learning. But I am equally distressed to see workshops on faculty development in which faculty exchange views about student learning with no reference to what scholars know through study of the matter" (Cross, 1998).

Developing her arguments through the 1990s, Cross consolidated her views on assessment and research in the classroom in two books, *Classroom Assessment Techniques: A Handbook for College Teachers* (with Thomas Angelo, 1993) and *Introduction to Classroom Research* (with Mimi Harris Steadman, 1996). College faculty could not be effective teachers unless they knew how to assess their teaching and their students' learning. There were, she believed, techniques—like the one-minute paper, learning logs, and student learning goals—that opened doors to what students learned in the classroom, doors that traditional forms of assessment like term papers and examinations only partially opened because they provided so little direct feedback as to be of almost no aid to either faculty or students. Feedback and classroom assessments should be immediate, constant, and converted into changes in practice for teaching to result in genuine improvements in student learning (Cross and Angelo, 1993). *Introduction to Classroom Research* (1996) summarized and extended these views by taking the rhetoric about the scholarship of teaching and giving it "operational definition." Since Cross believed the experiences of classroom teachers were the essential starting place for improvements in teaching and learning, she urged professors to engage in their own classroom research: observing students in the act of learning, reflecting and discussing observations and data with teaching colleagues, and reading the literature on learning. Determined to help faculty understand their teaching practices in order to improve student learning, Cross outlined the characteristics of classroom research:

- learner-centered: the attention of teachers and students is focused on observing and improving learning, rather than teaching;
- teacher-directed: classroom research changes the focus from teachers as consumers of research to teachers engaged in studies of learning in their discipline;
- collaborative: students and teachers are partners in the research on learning;
- context-specific: classroom research involves the teaching of a specific discipline to a particular group of students;
- scholarly: classroom research requires identifying a research question, developing and carrying out a research design (Cross and Steadman, 1996, pp. 2–3).

Cross' work on classroom assessment achieved widespread popularity. More than 50,000 copies of *Classroom Assessment Techniques* were sold. The American Association for Higher Education, in which she played an important role, increased its commitment to helping faculty and colleges in how to undertake classroom assessments. Numerous public and private universities and colleges, facing sharp criticisms from legislators and boards of trustees, concerned about their enrollments and retention rates, worried about the market consequences of dissatisfied families, and wanting to distinguish themselves as places where students learned, used Cross's ideas to initiate reforms.

More so than any other higher education reformer, Cross sought to shift the focus of the learning movement by bringing it directly into the classroom, ceaselessly presenting her ideas to higher education organizations and institutions, and, not insignificantly, developing a core of colleagues, like her co-authors Thomas Angelo and Mimi Harris Steadman, to extend her mission. She reiterated Boyer's view that teaching was a scholarly endeavor and made it concrete, showing how to undertake classroom research and continuous assessment. She thus used the status of research in an attempt to bring better teaching and improved learning to the classroom. Her arguments were both sweeping and concrete: faculty should understand and use research on learning; professors should understand the different motivations, academic backgrounds, and learning styles of their students; and they should carry out research in their classroom to improve their own teaching and students' learning.

But Cross' very concreteness, her emphasis on how to do it, made collegiate teaching and professors seem akin to secondary school teaching and teachers. There was an aura of teacher education and teacher professional development in both her approach and her tone, with the ironic result that her claim that teaching was an intellectual activity risked being displaced by instruction in teaching methods. Her approach thus found greater appeal to faculty and institutions that identified with the problems facing high school teachers than it did with those whose primary identifications were with disciplinary scholarship. Faculty and institutions that took their cues from graduate level work found Cross' proposals too close to secondary education to be comfortable. She was appealing to only part of the academic marketplace.

By the early 21st century, Cross had spent more than two decades making the case that teaching and learning were the heart of the academic enterprise and that there were concrete ways to improve both, if only faculty wanted to do so. Her work generated enormous enthusiasm to improve teaching and learning and yet seemed insufficiently connected to what many professors thought of as scholarly. What Cross had shown was that it lay in the faculty's power to improve the quality of their teaching and thereby to improve student learning. It was in the faculty's power if only they would take the responsibility. And, in that, her work cast a long shadow over higher education's traditional ways of doing things.

Connecting teaching to the disciplines: Lee Shulman

It was apparent that with the appointment of Stanford University's Lee Shulman to the presidency of the Carnegie Foundation for the Advancement of Teaching (CFAT), Ernest Boyer's efforts to create a scholarship of teaching would continue. For a number of years, Shulman had been calling for a tighter connection between the scholarly disciplines and the ways faculty taught. He believed that since the disciplines were themselves different, they should be taught differently. This meant that teaching was neither simply 'methodological'—good versus bad methods—nor just disciplinary—presenting students with information about history or chemistry—but a deeply embedded combination of both, what Shulman called "pedagogical content knowledge." The way one taught had to be varied by the discipline being taught. Shulman's goal, when he assumed CFAT's leadership, was thus simultaneously to extend Boyer's notion of teaching as a scholarly activity and to convert that rhetoric into improved teaching practice.

Shulman argued that teaching at all levels was not primarily a matter of learning the technique, an approach that he believed often dominated teacher education programs, but rather an enactment of teachers' understanding of their disciplines. Engaging in a wide range of teacher reform efforts, he came down on the side of teachers' disciplinary knowledge as the necessary condition of effective teaching, a theme he initially applied to high school teachers and teacher preparation. Given his commitment to disciplinary-based knowledge, it was a relatively easy step for Shulman to add higher education to the mix since, for most college teachers, their discipline was the starting point for their teaching.

Because Shulman was committed to moving the scholarship of teaching beyond rhetoric and into practice, he was at pains to define it, both as a form of scholarly endeavor and as a way to change teaching in the interests of student learning. Recognizing that the scholarship of teaching and teaching in the interests of learning were hard sells, Shulman seemed to be taking on what was an insurmountable endeavor. Writing in 1999, in an attempt to clarify their understanding of the issues, Patricia Hutchings and Shulman wrote:

> A scholarship of teaching is *not* synonymous with excellent teaching. It requires a kind of "going meta," in which faculty frame and systematically investigate questions related to student learning—the conditions under which it occurs, what it looks like, how to deepen it, and so forth—and so with an eye not only to improving their own classroom but to advancing practice beyond it. This conception of the scholarship of teaching is not something we presume all faculty (even the most excellent and scholarly teachers among them) will or should do—though it would be good to see that more of them have the opportunity to do so if they wish. But the scholarship of teaching *is* a condition—as yet a mostly absent condition—for excellent teaching. It is the mechanism through which the pro-

fession of teaching itself advances, through which teaching can be something other than a seat-of-the-pants operation, with each of us out there making it up as we go. As such, the scholarship of teaching has the potential to serve *all* teachers and students (Hutchings and Shulman, 1999, pp. 13–14. See also Shulman, 1999).

Using his position as head of the Carnegie Foundation for the Advancement of Teaching (CFAT), with the help of Pat Hutchings (formerly director of the American Association for Higher Education Teaching Initiative and Assessment Forum), Shulman established the Carnegie Teaching Academy in 1998 aimed at moving the scholarship of teaching from, as he put it, rhetoric to action. This six-million-dollar, five-year effort, funded by The Pew Charitable Trusts and CFAT, reinforced and extended what had by the end of the 1990s become the learning reformers' dominant *modus operandi*—the creation of a scholarship of teaching and learning, which would then improve the quality of student learning through new models of teaching and simultaneously raises the status of teaching itself.

The first of three components of the Carnegie Academy for the Scholarship of Teaching and Learning (CASTL) was a national fellowship program that brought together over a five-year-period 122 faculty, deemed "Carnegie Scholars," who were committed to inventing and sharing new conceptual models of teaching as scholarly work, to advance the profession of teaching, and to deepen students' learning. Participants were selected on the basis of prior engagement in investigating and documenting teaching practice and student learning, as well as in working with peers and in larger networks on the scholarship of teaching. Each scholar's project differed, from identifying the characteristics of a "good example" to assessing what students retained from science courses they completed. As a collectivity, CASTL's projects were intended to share five characteristics, including exploration of teacher practice and the resultant student learning and a commitment to the development of students. To show institutional commitments, each participant's campus had to contribute a release from 'campus duties'— clearly not wanting to call for a release from teaching in order to improve teaching—$3000 for travel expenses, and a commitment to bring the participant's work to the attention of others on campus.

The goal was to create a community of teaching scholars whose examples and missionary zeal could extend Shulman's aims.

The second component of CASTL was the Teaching Academy Campus Program for universities and colleges in all sectors of higher education that wanted to make a commitment to new models of teaching as scholarly work. This program was run jointly with AAHE with the long-term goal of engendering a national network of campuses that provided a structure, support, and forum for the scholarship of teaching and learning. The campus program was a multi-tiered set of activities designed to initiate and build toward a network of institutions that actually changed the definition and practice of teaching on their campuses. After conducting "campus conversations" about the scholarship of teaching as a problem to be studied "through materials appropriate to disciplinary epistemologies, application of results to practice, communication of results, reflection and peer review," institutions were expected to tailor this definition to their own situations and then select an area (or areas) for study and action, building on strengths, eliminating barriers, or bolstering campus ability to contribute to the scholarship of teaching and learning. Individual institutions quickly developed a variety of foci, exploring such issues as the effect of service learning on acquiring and generating disciplinary knowledge; intellectual property rights regarding syllabi, curricular materials, and web-based teaching materials; and instructional teams as curriculum builders. At a second stage institutions were expected to "go public," using $5,000 grants to open their work to a wider audience for feedback and consumption. In a third stage, selected institutions were invited to become members of a National Teaching Academy.

The final component of CASTL focused on collaboration with scholarly and professional societies. The goal was to spread the notion of teaching as embedded in the disciplines by working directly with disciplinary and professional organizations of academics. CASTL established a small-grants program to support activities such as the dissemination of examples of the scholarship of teaching and learning in the field, experiments with new outlets, and efforts aimed at making graduate programs in the field more responsive to new ideas about scholarly work.

In reviewing these efforts, the breadth of commitment and the care that went into planning and organizing them stands in stark contrast to the more typical reform activities of throwing the reform at potential recipients with a lot of hype and some money. Shulman and his colleagues genuinely believed in building a community of people interested in investigating and documenting teaching as scholarly work. By redefining "scholarly work" to include teaching, by supporting presentations at scholarly societies, and by helping create networks of teacher-scholars, there is little question that they raised the profile and helped create a new kind of infrastructure that supported higher education teaching. These successes reflected Shulman's goal to push the learning reform movement forward by adopting what is now the most common presumption of its protagonists from within higher education: reform will only occur when professors define teaching as a scholarly activity, seek to understand it as such, and revise their practices in light of research on teaching and learning.

Simple to state, difficult to create. Shulman had shifted his early emphasis on getting elementary and high schools and teacher education programs to pay attention to disciplinary-based teaching to an emphasis on getting colleges and universities to take student learning seriously. It was an extremely hard task. There is certainly some evidence that the profile of teaching on campuses was raised during the years that Shulman headed the Carnegie Foundation for the Advancement of Teaching. But perhaps more telling, when Shulman stepped down as head of the Foundation in 2008, his replacement was another Stanford professor whose primary interest had always been elementary and secondary schools. CFAT, for the first time in its more than 100-year-history seemingly had shifted its attention away from higher education, calling into question Shulman's (and Ernest Boyer's) agenda. Although CFAT moved to focus on teaching in community colleges, the shift signaled the loss of steam in the teaching and learning revolution.

6.4 The reformers' dilemma

Understanding how and why things happen illuminates the nature of the debates and the attempts at reform. Understanding that the assessment movement was the result of the drive for accountability at the national and state levels—and *not* the result of local campus initiatives to improve teaching and learning—sheds light on why the assessment movement's reform efforts were framed as demands and threats to colleges and universities that they show better performance. A genuine conversation on how to improve student learning, however, depended upon a more intimate understanding of the complexities and realities of higher education's value structure, depended more upon conversion and beliefs than heavy handed threats. The teaching and learning reformers understood that. They believed that higher education had indeed lost its way and that an industry that depended upon the dreams of millions to get ahead was self destructing by adhering to a status and reward system that subordinated collegiate teaching and student learning to research and the authority of the academic disciplines. Their views pointed to a deeper failure: Higher education's value and reward system did not require professors to take more than minimal responsibility for student learning and student development. Enlarging the importance of teaching and expecting improved learning from students was in fact an opportunity to revise higher education's system of values.

The learning reformers started by using the research reward system itself as an avenue for change. If definitions of research could be expanded to encompass a scholarship of teaching, designed to aid professors improve the learning of their students, the very reward system that dominated and warped higher education could be effectively used in its reform. Boyer's pleas to give teaching greater scholarly status, Cross' efforts to show how one could undertake classroom research and assessment to improve teaching and student learning, and Shulman's models of teaching based on disciplinary knowledge were all designed to re-conceptualize professors' work along the lines that academically-oriented faculty could appreciate. The arguments were, in many ways, brilliant: Professors cared about teaching, but lacked the tools and the incentives to teach better and to take greater responsibility for student learning. If the reformers could show faculty that research into how their students learned could be genuinely fulfilling and rewarded, it could foster widespread support where it matters—from within the professorial community itself.

During the 1980s and 1990s and into the 21st century, the official organizations of higher education joined the chorus. The American Association for Higher Education, prodded by close relationships to the reformers, took up the argument that higher education's value and reward system was at odds with the central obligations of teaching and student learning. AAHE undertook a series of projects on assessments and faculty roles designed to help colleges and universities make the assessment of student learning congruent with faculty values. In addition to hosting national conventions, workshops, and symposia, AAHE's journal, *Change*, under the editorship of Theodore Marchese, regularly published articles on assessment, new ways of teaching, and learning reforms. The Carnegie Foundation for the Advancement of Teaching regularly convened panels and meetings of scholars that resulted in reports such as *Scholarship Reconsidered* (Boyer, 1990) and *Scholarship Assessed* (Glassick, et al., 1997).

Although the rhetoric of the learning reformers became widely used, documented improvements in teaching and student learning do not seem to have occurred. Boyer's conception of a scholarship of teaching received enormous national attention, but it neither reshaped college and university campuses nor altered traditional teaching practices. While Cross' classroom assessment techniques achieved considerable popularity, reforms have primarily occurred within limited sectors of higher education, and their breadth and depth seem questionable. Her insistence that faculty engage in classroom research as a way to improve learning posed a serious threat to most professors' usual way of doing business. It appears to have had little impact on colleges and universities that continue to place scholarship at the forefront of their reward system, although individual professors seem to use her 'one-minute' end-of-class summaries. Shulman's programs, while supported with substantial funding, were too often based on the premise "we will give opportunities to reformers and they will teach the rest," an uncertain foundation from which to initiate change in an industry or an organization.

The learning revolution thus seems far away, replaced by a new wave of reform based on a technological imperative that, if enough technology is used, students will truly learn more; the era of Power Point and web-based interactive distance learning is upon us. Assessment, outcomes, value-added are now buzz words on campuses, even as they lack any serious connection to teaching practices and faculty rewards. There may be a certain amount of campus conversations on alternative approaches to teaching and the assessment of student learning, but there also appears to be little dialogue of substance and implementation of reforms at most colleges and universities that would enhance student learning. The slogan "involvement in learning" is widely bandied about in a variety of forms, and there are hundreds of active classrooms where students take responsibility for their learning. But such efforts have not yet led to serious assessments of student learning; the internet itself, although in constant use by students, is often seen as a threat by professors—witness the outcry over Wikipedia's accuracy even as it has become the students' research tool of choice. Most strikingly, there have been few real changes in a value and reward system that remains fixated on faculty research and scholarly production, although many colleges and universities insist that teaching evaluations be part of faculty review for promotion and tenure.

The rhetoric and the limited changes suggest that the efforts to change teaching and improve learning are actually battles over institutional values and rewards. Almost all the signals of the last decades said that scholarly productivity and research grants gave the institution value and brought rewards to professors—promotion, tenure, higher salary, and prestige in the free-agent marketplace. Gradients exist in the broad spectrum of colleges and universities, but even many of the institutions that define their primary mission as teaching give research grants and publications high status. For faculty who want to make teaching and student learning the centerpiece of their existence, little institutional support exists. Professors remain connected to their disciplines; they teach subject matter and assess the students' levels of knowledge through tests and papers, sometimes projects and classroom participation, and give out grades.

They are highly resistant to efforts to make them more responsible for students' learning and hostile to external agencies that make demands, including even their own university's administration. The pressure to change is blunted by the continuing student demand for higher education. The classroom continues to be treated as a private domain protected by academic freedom; "thou shalt not enter" continues to be a professorial prerogative. While there are a spate of institutional and some national awards recognizing outstanding teaching, and some professors have achieved prominence for analyzing why their students were not learning and then modifying their teaching, the recognition has done little to revise institutional cultures.

The values/rewards dilemma is exacerbated by the continuing influence of the origins of the learning reform movement. Initiated by fiscal concerns and criticism of higher education's organizational and governance structures, the reform of teaching and learning was initially seen by external bodies as a way to hold institutions accountable and to establish a basis upon which to make budgetary allocations. As state legislatures and governors concluded that their imposition of student assessment was neither leading to greater accountability nor were the results aiding them in their fiscal decisions, they quickly shifted to performance outcomes that were relatively simple to measure and to compare across institutions: retention and graduation rates, scores on standardized professional tests, acceptance rates into graduate schools, alumni salaries, student-faculty ratios and contact hours. The goal continues to be to hold higher education accountable for the funds it receives and the effect seems largely to be professorial resistance to taking responsibility for student learning seriously.

There are at least two other continuing dilemmas that face the efforts to improve teaching and learning. The first is simply the problem of imitation and the hostility of most graduate departments preparing future professors. Most new professors more or less imitate what they remember of their professors' modes of teaching. In the best of circumstances, they choose to build upon the best of the professorial instructors—but even when they try to innovate, the weight of decades of schooling in which instructors talked at students, who had to learn what they were being told, is too great to overcome. This is exacerbated by graduate programs that do not take their students' future roles as teaching professors all that seriously. The road to professorial success in the academy, and certainly at the elite institutions, remains research productivity. Why would you teach doctoral students how to teach, when they are going to get faculty jobs, promotions, and tenure largely based on their research?

The second dilemma is, unfortunately, barely noticed. Or, if it is, the recognition of it usually comes in the form of complaints about the wired generation, the instant gratification generation, the 'is it going to get me a job' generation—take your pick. As Rebecca Cox (2009) has shown, the gap is huge even between those instructors seeking to engage their students in learning, hoping that they will take away from the engagement ways of thinking about issues, able to distinguish among different pieces of evidence, and aware of complexity and their students, who often have very narrow definitions of "real" instruction and "useful" knowledge. Students and professors may misunderstand one another in fundamental ways that can only be overcome with a great deal of commitment and energy on both sides. The view, too often still held by those in higher education, that faculty are there to teach their subjects and then get out of the way of the students so that they can learn and complete their tasks, retains much of its traditional power—over both students and faculty.

Still, if the revolution has not occurred, the rumblings about learning have become too loud to ignore, especially as colleges and universities find themselves in intense competition for students. Community colleges, faced with growing competition from open access four-year institutions and from for-profit distance education suppliers and seeing students go through revolving doors, entering and leaving with regularity, are looking for ways to connect the college more tightly to job markets, to improve transfer programs to four-year schools, and to create more sustainable learning environments. Four-year institutions are worrying about high incompletion rates, students who simply disappear, at substantial fiscal cost to the school, whose failure to graduate lowers the institution's ranking and raises a red flag to public officials and accreditation agencies about educational quality. In response, they are instituting early identification and intervention programs for students experiencing academic difficulties and trying to connect those programs to learning. Learning and writing centers have been increasing in number, as have writing sections connected to departments and individual courses. Highly selective institutions are modifying their self-descriptions to show that they are more student-learner centered than their rivals. Almost in spite of itself, higher education has been driven to experiment with learning. Residential and non-residential institutions are trying out "learning communities" to connect faculty and students in the pursuit of improved learning. Efforts at curricular reform include rethinking general education and core requirements and introducing and expanding interdisciplinary majors. Student portfolios to assess student learning continue to have some saliency, although the optimism of two decades ago has not yielded fruit. Teaching experiments receive administrative support, at least when there is no financial crisis. A number of campus teaching centers and awards for teaching exist. Competency-based learning in health education has extended to other areas. And, growing rapidly, distance education and the use of interactive technology may challenge the most sacrosanct traditions of teaching and learning. There is no revolution, but maybe there is hope for improvement.

Part IV
Making Things Better

CHAPTER 7

Why is higher education so hard to reform?

I can't get no satisfaction. And I try.
(The Rolling Stones)

Americans' faith in the power of education to cure everything is all-encompassing. This gospel of education asserts that social, economic, political, and ethical problems can be solved through schooling. Whatever the difficulties and the aspirations—economic development *and* individual economic success, social instability *and* social security, global competition *and* national identity, intolerance *and* tolerance, religious *and* secular values, economic productivity *and* satisfaction at work, the list could go on and on—the Education Gospel assumes that schooling can solve the problem and meet the goals.

The essential message connected to such terms as 'knowledge society', 'information society', and high-tech revolution' is that life in the 21st century will require people with skills associated with knowledge and information, and that these can best be learned in schools, especially the skills that come with college education and beyond. In the face of intense global competition, the need to make decisions about complex problems, to preserve democracy, and to bring ethical behavior and tolerance into a world that often seems to reward the opposite, as well as enhancing each individual's chances at professional status, economic success, and social security, mass schooling is absolutely necessary. It assures economic growth and democracy.

In the United States, the gospel of education has produced remarkable results. America has provided more schooling for more people sooner and for longer periods of time than any other country. Millions of immigrants and their families, millions of poor and working class, millions of previously discriminated against can attest to the remarkable openness and opportunities available through education. Faith in the Education Gospel lies at the heart of America's belief in itself. It is one of the givens of the American Dream.

The problem with the Gospel is not the faith itself, but rather its exaggeration, its tendency to deny the importance of so many other aspects of global, national, and individual existence. Schools are not always the best places to learn about life, and certainly not the exclusive places to learn about work. And, because the Gospel has in the last decades become so closely attached to economic success for the nation and for individuals, it has become a distorting lens through which education is seen primarily—often exclusively—as a transmission belt. One goes to school in order to get to the next level of schooling. Schooling's value lies in its payoffs; the more schooling, the larger expected payoffs.

This exaggerated faith leads to a continuing condition of dissatisfaction, since schools simply cannot accomplish all that Americans expect of it, and certainly not for all the people who spend time in school. At best, the expectations can only be partially realized, leading to an environment in which proposals to change, reform, or punish schools are a way of life, leading to constant tampering with education, with the misguided hope that there is a right recipe that just has to be put in place. The tampering is almost always initiated from outside schools at every level, from kindergarten through graduate education. Constantly badgered by yet another attempt at reform or more accurately, by multiple reforms simultaneously, those within schools—teachers, professors, administrators—more often than not hold the line. They both believe in what they are doing and they understand that in a short period of time yet another set of reforms will be on the agenda. The first step, then, in improving education is to see it as one of many institutions and policy options available for economic growth, social progress, and individual success. Education is important—very important—but there are so many other things that have to be improved if education is to come closer to achieving its aspirations.

7.1 Money matters—if used correctly

Higher education's success has been built on its ability to gain a near monopoly on access to the American Dream. The monopoly is not total; the media provides the occasional story about the self-made individual who made it without much schooling, but the occasions are rare. Colleges and universities have taken over the preparation of skilled labor, the provision of expert knowledge, and scientific research. That success has brought with it millions and millions of dollars from public and private sources. Higher education's success in attracting money stimulates the desire for even more money. The search for gold has become an ever-present phenomenon. It is the dominating characteristic of American higher education. In the words of Harvard's former president, Derek Bok:

> Universities learned that they could sell the right to use their scientific discoveries to industry and find corporations willing to pay a tidy sum to sponsor courses delivered by Internet or cable television. Apparel firms offered money to have colleges place the corporate logo on their athletic uniforms or, conversely, to put the university's name on caps and sweatshirts sold to the public. Faculty members began to bear such titles as Yahoo Professor of Computer Science or K-Mart Professor of Marketing (Bok, 2003, pp. 1–2).

This phenomenon of selling one's self is not new, but the size, the amounts, and the intensity of the last few decades are. The amounts that became and remain available are staggering. What was once a story of survival—we need funds to keep going—or about selected investments—our faculty and students need laboratories—has become a focus on profits. In Bok's words, the commercialization of higher education refers to efforts "to make a profit from teaching, research, and other campus activities" (Bok, 2003, p.3; see also Kirp, 2003).

Money is not a bad thing. Without funding from external sources, the cost of going to college would rise even more precipitously than it has, and higher education would likely return to a much more limited enterprise, cutting off large numbers of young people and adults from the opportunities it provides. Without external funding, research would revert to industrial and commercial laboratories, where potential income returns and secrecy would dominate every step of the research process. Few of us would think that would be a good thing for society.

Still the ceaseless desire for money has an obscene quality to it, in part because profit often seems to become an end in itself, rather than a genuine attempt to improve the quality of education. Profit as an end in itself makes higher education look little different than other industries. There are other disturbing aspects. The availability of money has made it difficult to make hard decisions about what is and is not important. The tendency has been to build and to add on without serious consideration of what is no longer working well, what is no longer worth doing, and what can and needs to be changed. Greater income converts into more expenditure without a clear sense of what should no longer be done. In the years leading up to the financial crisis of 2008–09, colleges and universities of every shape and form used the funds they received to start new projects, institute new kinds of programs, create more attractive settings for students and professors without taking seriously what needs to disappear, be modified, or dramatically improved. Hard decisions were in short supply, because the goal was often to spend money without eliciting conflict.

The recent financial crisis appears to have modified that, but appearances can be deceiving. Cutting jobs, freezing new appointments, closing programs, unpaid furloughs, postponing capital investments and delaying needed maintenance are emotionally difficult and, for the people directly affected, painful. But such decisions, taken under intense pressure to balance budgets, do not necessarily lead to rethinking what really matters or where the resources, when they return, should be invested. The sad story of having money over the last decades was the tendency to spend rather than think through what the institution should be about. Whether the latter will occur in the coming decades remains an open question, but unless attitudes fundamentally change, the likelihood is high that higher education will revert back to the same patterns of the last few decades. Maybe it will even get worse, since the panic of not having money remains, further intensify the desire to gather even more than in the past.

An alternative is for higher education to take note of the mounting research on learning and the financing of elementary and secondary education. Here, the evidence is clear: money matters. Anyone who says it does not when it comes to learning is either an idiot or a liar. Yes, there is excellent teaching and a lot of learning occurring in very poorly-funded schools, colleges, and universities, but the differences in teaching conditions, learning environments, and retention rates are often so dramatic compared to affluent institutions that huge successes, when they occur, are extraordinary occurrences. Without money, instructors are poorly-paid, better facilities are not built and existing ones deteriorate, and the technology and supplies necessary to learning are unavailable. Money is necessary, but it also not sufficient.

What W. Norton Grubb (2009, p. xii) has written with regard to elementary and secondary schooling applies also to higher education: "leadership, vision, cooperation among teachers, effective instruction, unbiased information about effective versus ineffective practices, stability, consistent district and state policies—are necessary as well." And, if money is to be used effectively to improve learning, it and the other resources have to be focused on the educational process itself and not on ancillary activities. For higher education, this may be even more difficult than in elementary and secondary schools. The latter have fundamental learning responsibilities, and while these are often supplemented with a variety of extra-curricula activities and social development responsibilities, the fact is, that schools cannot escape the expectation that children and youth will learn in them. The involvement by parents in their children's educational lives, as well as the political (and scholarly) attention drawn to how well children are (and are not) learning in elementary and secondary schools is one measure that learning is the 'bottom line', the way to decide whether a school or classroom is functioning or not.

For universities and colleges, the question of learning is murkier. With many faculty supposed to be researchers and with many colleges and universities making research productivity the essential requirement of appointment, promotion, and tenure, the question of how much students are actually learning receives less attention. Traditions of disciplinary-based knowledge—one is a historian not a teacher—combined with the strongly held belief by college and university instructors that the classroom is a private domain protected by academic freedom have made it extremely difficult to intervene on behalf of improved instruction, leaving higher education leaders wary of intervening to improve teaching and learning. Added to this, almost no one in higher education takes seriously research findings on students' learning. If elementary and secondary education has suffered from repeated waves of reforms, with new ones showing up in a continuing fashion, higher education has manifested the opposite condition. Most ideas on how to improve learning are simply ignored; the reigning ideology, even with the various student support systems that have been created, is that the students who enter colleges and universities have a responsibility to learn. If they do not, they suffer the consequences.

Still the evidence that students can learn more than they are currently is there, and if some of it were injected into colleges and universities, financial investments might flow in a better direction than in the past. Here are a few suggestions[1]:

– Emphasize instruction. This turns out to be simple to say and hard to do, because it would require breaking ranks with the rhetoric and practice that exalts and rewards everything else—from research through athletics. It requires providing genuine rewards for good teaching and not as add-ons to the reward system, i.e. as in everything stays the same, but we are adding some "outstanding teacher awards" in the form of a gift certificate to the bookstore and a plaque. And, it would provide incentives for cooperative teaching, again not as adjuncts to budgets, but as a fundamental expectation that it is worth funding more than other things.

– Create more personalized learning environments. Helping students gain a stake in what they are learning, enabling them to cooperate with one another, developing a sense of trust about learning between instructors and students through learning communities, living and learning residential programs, majors within majors that allow small groups of students to distinguish themselves from the hundreds of departmental or programmatic majors.

---

[1] These are drawn from Grubb (2009). Although Grubb's book is focused on elementary and secondary education, a number of his findings and recommendations directly or indirectly apply to higher education. I have refocused them as appropriate.

– Expand the notion of professional education. Higher education has become dominated by professional education, with the vast number of undergraduates enrolled in pre-professional programs and almost all graduate programs being explicitly professional education. The tendency of pre-professional and professional education to narrow themselves, with more and more focus on the technical aspects of each profession is disheartening. The response, however, is not to tamper, once again, with general education, as a distinct category, a separate and, to many students, irrelevant adjunct to professional education. Rather the response should be to figure out how to bring meaningful intellectual, conceptual, philosophical, and ethical issues into professional education—and I mean genuinely incorporated into the core of what it means to be a professional.

These proposals seem so obvious that their absence, beyond the frequent rhetorical flights of fancy about the commitment to student learning, poses serious questions about whether higher education really cares about learning, which is at the heart of what needs to be changed. The recommendations also require money, which means that institutions that are financially poor will have more difficulty implementing them than those with access to money. Unfortunately the overriding inequalities in the financing of higher education institutions cannot be overcome without dramatic changes in public policy. Still every institution that genuinely wants its students to learn can take steps to do so, showing a willingness to reallocate money to where it really matters, rather than wait for the new money to come in so that learning can be added to the agenda.

7.2 Stop the loud music

When I was growing up my father and grandfather worked in a New York City factory. In order to hear themselves over the noise of the machinery, they had to shout. Of course, all the others around them were also shouting, so they learned to shout even more loudly. This shouting as the basic form of conversation continued when they sat down at the dinner table. One consequence of this, was that in order to make myself heard I too shouted, often more loudly than they did. One younger sister joined in the shouting. A second sister, considerably younger than the two of us, responded over the years by leaving the dinner table screaming.

My reaction to all of this noise, since there was no such thing as a conversation, was to go to my room, and turn on a New York City radio station that was introducing its listeners to rhythm and blues, what soon became known as rock and roll. I turned the music up very loudly, which of course led to more shouting, a sister playing her music more loudly, and my grandfather and father turning the sound up on the family television—and in the paper-thin walls of a Levitt house in the 1950s, every sound could be heard, if not understood.

Over the years, I began to think about my family in the context of educational reform. What became clear to me is that the advocates of educational reform, from all sides of the political spectrum, behave like my family did—shout and play loud music, with each participant or each supporter of 'whatever' turning up the sound. Since at least one group of reformers is always shouting, other reformers have to shout even more loudly to be heard, leading to seemingly unending rounds of loudly played music.

In these situations, no one can really hear anyone's music, so everyone simply stops listening and becomes highly effective and efficient at screening out all forms of music except for one's own. Over the years this has left us with almost no capacity to listen to anyone but ourselves and our friends, and it has utterly demolished our ability to engage in serious conversations about education. In higher education, it essentially means that very little ever really changes and that when change occurs, it often exists in a kind of parallel universe. One group gets what it wants, while the others continue to have what they previously had. A colleague once said to me that he had lived through 6 or 7 provosts at the university, each of them 'reform-minded', but as far as he could see, his life as a professor had stayed almost exactly the same—we are talking here about a 30-year stretch. In this context, it makes little difference what educational researchers, public officials, administrators and professors, or students say, since the music is so blaring that people more or less only hear what they already believe to be true.

There is little in the way of serious conversations, although there is a lot of shouting.

Things are not going to get better and reform will not really occur unless the competing players lower the music, limit the shouting, and stop acting as if what they have to say is the only thing that matters. Until that happens, no one really hears anything. For colleges and universities that is a tragedy.

7.3 There are no silver bullets

Next to The Shadow, which was introduced by Orson Welles, my favorite radio program as a child was The Lone Ranger. In contrast to playing rock and roll loudly, I would keep the Lone Ranger radio program quiet, not wanting my parents to know that I was in bed with my ears glued to the radio for the stirring overture that introduced the program. As I moved from the 1950s into the 1960s, and the Lone Ranger had moved to television, I understood that this white man who wore a mask was politically incorrect. White men just did not have faithful Indian companions named Tonto. But in the 1950s, the Lone Ranger was one of my outlets to a world beyond my family.

There were always two stirring moments in the program. One came at the very end, when someone who had been helped by the Lone Ranger would ask: "Who is that masked man?" A voice would answer, "that's the Lone Ranger" and over the music would come a voice, "hi ho Silver"—Silver was the Lone Ranger's horse. The other stirring moment came early in the show and was much more interesting to me, for it meant that the real action was about to begin. It was when someone would notice the Lone Ranger's bullets, and would say, "why those are silver bullets, mister." That meant, that the Lone Ranger was on the case and the action would begin.

Through years of talking with Patricia A. Graham about education, I became reacquainted with silver bullets, for Graham would hold firmly to the position that as long as educational reformers kept searching and believing in instant cures, like medical researchers looking for the antibiotic, vaccine, or gene that would eliminate the disease, our educational problems would not be solved. The Lone

Ranger's silver bullets were just that, since they never missed their mark and they always landed where the Lone Ranger wanted them to.

Americans treat educational reform much like the Lone Ranger's silver bullets, and they have for a long time. What is relatively new has been the application of silver bullets to higher education reform. In the last few decades, the number of simple resolutions to complex problems looks a lot like the Lone Ranger's approach: eliminate the problem within a half-hour, including commercial breaks. The accountability movement of the 1980s, the increased wave of accreditation efforts, the 'let's make teaching a scholarly activity', the repeated efforts to amend general education, the growth of interdisciplinary studies, a bewildering array of new programs and new technologies—all get presented as if these were the breakthroughs. But unlike medical research, there are few if any breakthroughs in education, which is a slow, sometimes painful, sometimes joyful process that requires constant effort and attention, and whose payoffs are always down the road. We rarely know what we have accomplished until many years later, and even then, we can never be sure how much was education's doing.

One of the best things we can do is to bury the belief that any single reform, even one we very much believe in, is going to do all that much. Education is a complex business and many things need to happen to improve it. Silver bullets just don't make it and the Lone Ranger could not possibly have shot so perfectly. Even when we are on the right track, education takes a long time to have an effect. Learning does not occur overnight. And so, we have a responsibility to say as clearly as we can, that what we want to do may help some if we do it right, but no reform is a silver bullet that will make the educational problem disappear. Sorry, Lone Ranger.

7.4 How about playing within your game

One of the saddest aspects of U.S. higher education is the "wan-a-be" phenomenon, the desire, wish, and impulse to be like the other place, especially if the other place has a higher reputation, more money, and greater status than you do. One sees this in a variety of circumstances. Local and regional colleges and universities that admit the overwhelming majority of applicants, whose students are overwhelmingly from a relatively circumscribed geographic area, who are overwhelmingly enrolled in professional programs, continue to describe themselves as the 'Harvard of the region', make faculty appointments of graduates of the big research universities, declare how important it is that their professors be researchers, and talk incessantly about their international connections. None of this, taken singly, is bad. Why not aspire to emulate Harvard? Why not recruit professors from the best doctoral programs in the U.S.? Why not make research the primary decider of promotion and tenure? Taken together, however, such efforts at emulation miss the possibilities of being powerful teaching institutions and serious contributors to the skilled labor market and social and economic development in the neighborhoods and region within which the institution lives.

I was reminded of this during the summer of 2004, when I watched the European Soccer Championships. Like soccer's World Cup, the European championships involve an initial series of qualifying rounds that occur over the course of almost 2 years. The actual championships begin with round robins involving a small group of teams, with the top teams in each group entering the final round. The final games, like the NCAA basketball tournament, are one loss and you are out variety. As the qualifying round robin got under-way—indeed in the opening game against highly favored Portugal—the national team from Greece began to win games it was supposed to lose. This was surprising, as every soccer commentator noted, because the Greeks had no superstars. Indeed, the player who emerged as Greece's best goal scorer during the tournament was not even in the starting line-up for the German soccer club he played for during the regular season. Pretty soon, everybody started to take the Greek team seriously, and attention turned to the team's German coach, who, it was said, had convinced his players to "play within their game." Well, playing within their game worked for the Greeks, and in one of the biggest surprises ever in European soccer, the national team of Greece became the European champions.

For those of you who are not sport fans, the phrase "playing within your game" probably doesn't mean anything. Others will recognize it as a shorthand phrase that essentially means that a team of not especially great players has learned to draw upon and combine its individual strengths to make for strong team play. Playing within your game says that these players *taken together* are stronger as a team than the individual parts. Parenthetically, this is now a relatively rare characteristic of professional sports in the U.S., where individual superstars determine the character of teams.

Many colleges and universities have no idea what it is to play within your game. In fact, most of them have no game plan other than looking like the reputed better, more affluent, higher status institution down the road, around the corner, in a different part of the state, or in some other section of the country. Even community colleges, whose very existence lies in their capacity to aid students in gaining access to skilled labor markets and local four-year colleges or universities, talk about becoming four-year bachelor degree granting institutions. A lot of effort thus gets put into becoming something one is not rather than being really good at what you are. The "wan-a-be" phenomenon means that institutions are constantly looking somewhere else for their models of what they should be. In the end, too many institutions have no real purpose other than to be like something else. This means there is insufficient attention or opportunity to build upon and blend an institution's strengths to make it a better place to be. The notion of playing within your game in order to make the institution better is almost an oxymoron. It hardly ever exists.

7.5 It is hard to be really good when conditions are so unequal

It would be a mistake to think that all institutions can achieve high levels of performance simply on their own. The inequalities of wealth make that impossible. The differences are substantial.

In 2000–2001, research universities in California spent $16,293 per student for instructional purposes. The amount spent per student at the state colleges was $10,787 and at the community colleges, with the greatest variety of students and the greatest challenges, $4,606 was spent per student. The amounts reported undoubtedly underplay the differences, since the research universities spent considerably more on none instructional items than the state colleges and community colleges (Grubb and Lazerson, 2004, p. 73).

Nationally, for data also covering 2000–01, (National Center for Educational Statistics, 2002, Table 342), spending per full-time equivalent student varied from \$32,512 in research universities to \$17,780 in public doctoral institutions to \$11,345 in public universities granting master's degrees to \$7,665 in community colleges. This more than four-fold difference between the per student expenditures attests to the fact that while almost everybody can go to some college, one is not treated equally, and those with the most difficulty in school are treated less equally than the others.

The financial differences reveal that higher education bets on winners and losers in the race to the American Dream. It offers itself as the route to the Dream, but it does so in highly stratified ways. Who will have access to which colleges and to which degrees and who will have the kind of support that converts access into achievement remain too closely connected to one's origins to be brushed under the rug of "everyone in America has the opportunity to go to college." Higher education does provide access to the American Dream, but it does so in divided ways that will continue to be contested, controversial, and lead to political confrontations over its behavior. The extraordinary successes mean that our expectations for higher education will continue to grow, and with that will come further discontentment.

References

Abrams, M. H. (1997). "The Transformation of English Studies: 1930–1995." *Daedalus* 126 (Winter): 105–131.

Ackerman, Bruce (1991). *We the People: Foundations*. Cambridge: Harvard University Press.

——— (1998). *We the People: Transformations*. Cambridge: Harvard University Press.

Aper, Jeffrey P. and Dennis E. Hinkle (1991). "State Policies for Assessing Student Outcomes: A Case Study with Implications for State and Institutional Authorities." *Journal of Higher Education* 62. No. 5.

Altbach, Philip G., Liz Reisberg, and Laura E. Rumbley (2009). *Trends in Global Higher Education: Tracking an Academic Revolution*. Chestnut Hill, MA: Center for International Higher Education, Boston College.

Association of American Colleges (1985). *Integrity in the College Curriculum: A Report to the Academic Community*. Washington, D.C.: Association of American Colleges.

Astin, Alexander W. (1985a). *Achieving Educational Excellence*. San Francisco: Jossey-Bass.

——— (1985b). "Involvement: The Cornerstone of Excellence." *Change* (July/August): 35–39.

Bannister, Robert C. (1987). *Sociology and Scientism: The American Quest for Objectivity, 1880–1940*. Chapel Hill: University of North Carolina Press.

Banta, Trudy W. and Associates (1993). *Making a Difference: Outcomes of a Decade of Assessment in Higher Education*. San Francisco: Jossey-Bass Publishers.

Barber, William J. (1997). "Reconfigurations in American Academic Economics: A General Practitioner's Perspective." *Daedalus* 126 (Winter 1997): 87–103.

Bell, Daniel (1982). *The Social Sciences Since the Second World War*. New Brunswick, NJ: Transaction Books.

Bender, Thomas (1986). "Wholes and Parts: The Need for Synthesis in American History." *Journal of American History* 73 (1986): 120–136.

——— (1997). "Politics, Intellect, and the American University, 1945–1995." *Daedalus* 126 (Winter 1997): 1–38.

Bennett, William John (1984). *To Reclaim a Legacy: A Report on the Humanities in Higher Education*. Washington, D.C.: National Endowment for the Humanities.

Bird, Caroline (1975). *The Case Against College*. New York: David McKay.

Blumberg, Paul (1980). *Inequality in an Age of Decline*. New York: New York University Press.

Bok, Derek (1986). "Toward Higher Learning: The Importance of Assessing Outcomes." *Change*. November/December, 18–27.

——— (1990). *Scholarship Reconsidered: Priorities of the Professoriate*. Princeton: Carnegie Foundation for the Advancement of Teaching.

——— (2003). *Universities in the Marketplace: the Commercialization of Higher Education*. Princeton: Princeton University Press.

——— (2007). *Our Underachieving Colleges: A Candid Look at How Much Students Learn and Why They Should be Learning More*. Princeton: Princeton University Press.

Boyer, Ernest L. (1987). *College: The Undergraduate Experience in America*. New York: Harper and Row.

——— (1990). *Scholarship Reconsidered: Priorities of the Professoriate*. Princeton: Carnegie Foundation fot the Advancement of Teaching.

Brainard, Jeffrey, Paul Fain, and Kathryn Masterson (2009). "Support Staff Jobs Double in 20 Years, Outpacing Enrollment." *Chronicle of Higher Education*, April 24.

Bransford, John D., Ann L. Brown, Ann L., and Rodney R. Cocking, ed. (1999). *How People Learn: Brain, Mind, Experience, and School*. Committee on Developments in the Science of Learning, Commission on Behavioral and Social Sciences and

Education, National Research Council. Washington, D.C.: National Academy Press.

Breneman, David W. (1994). *Liberal Arts Colleges: Thriving or Endangered?* Washington, D.C.: Brookings Institution.

Brint, S. (2002). "The Rise of the 'Practical Arts'." In S. Brint, ed., *The Future of the City of Intellect: The Changing American University.* Stanford: Stanford University.

Brint, S. and J. Karabel (1989). *The Diverted Dream.* New York: Oxford University Press.

Burke, Joseph C. and Andreea M. Serban (1998a). "Funding Public Higher Education for Results: Fad or Trend? Results from the Second Annual Survey." *Rockefeller Reports.* The Nelson A. Rockefeller Institute of Government, State University of New York, July 24.

————— (1998b). "Performance Funding for Public Higher Education: Fad or Trend?" *New Directions for Institutional Research.* No. 97. San Francisco: Jossey-Bass Publishers.

Carnochan, W. B. (1993). *The Battleground of the Curriculum: Liberal Education and the American Experience.* Stanford: Stanford University Press.

Chait, Richard (1995). *The New Activism of Corporate Boards and the Implications for Campus Governance.* Association of Governing Boards of Universities and Colleges: Occasional Paper, #26.

Chait, Richard and Thomas P. Holland (1996). "The New Work of the Nonprofit Board." *Harvard Business Review,* Sept/Oct.

Clark, Burton R. (1987). *The Academic Life: Small Worlds, Different Worlds.* Princeton, NJ: Carnegie Foundation for the Advancement of Teaching.

Clowse, Barbara Barksdale (1981). *Brainpower for the Cold War: The Sputnik Crisis and National Defense Education Act of 1958.* Westport, CT: Greenwood Press.

Colby, Anne, Elizabeth Beaumont, Thomas Ehrlich and Josh Corngold (2007). Education for Democracy: *Preparing Undergraduates for Responsible Political Engagement.* San Francisco: Jossey-Bass.

Cox, Rebecca D. (2009). *The College Fear Factor: How Students and Professors Misunderstand One Another.* Cambridge: Harvard University Press.

Cross, K. Patricia (1971). *Beyond the Open Door.* San Francisco: Jossey-Bass Publishers.

———— (1976). *Accent on Learning.* San Francisco: Jossey-Bass Publishers.

———— (1981). *Adults as Learners: Increasing Participation and Facilitating Learning.* San Francisco: Jossey-Bass Publishers.

———— (1998). "What Do We Know about Students' Learning and How Do We Know It?" AAHE's National Conference on Higher Education.

Cross, K. Patricia and Thomas Angelo (1993). *Classroom Assessment Techniques: A Handbook for College Teachers.* San Francisco: Jossey-Bass Publishers.

Cross, K. Patricia and Mimi Harris Steadman (1996). *Classroom Research: Implementing the Scholarship of Teaching.* San Francisco: Jossey-Bass Publishers.

Cuban, Larry (1999). *How Scholars Trumped Teachers: The Paradox of Constancy and Change in University Curriculum, Research, and Teaching, 1890–1990.* Stanford: Stanford University Press.

Divine, Robert A. (1993). *The Sputnik Challenge.* New York: Oxford University Press.

Dougherty, Kevin. (1994). *The Contradictory College: The Conflicting Origins, Impacts, and Futures of the Community College.* Albany: State University of New York Press.

Dumont, Richard G. (1980). "Performance Funding and Power Relations in Higher Education." *Journal of Higher Education* 51, No. 4.

Ehrenberg, Ronald G. (2000). *Tuition Rising: Why College Costs So Much.* Cambridge: Harvard University Press.

Elkana, Yehuda (2005). "Unmasking Uncertainties, Embracing Contradictions" in Chris M. Golde, George E. Walker and Associates, *Preparing Stewards of the Disciplines: Carnegie Essays on the Doctorate.* San Francisco: Jossey-Bass.

Elmore, Richard F. and Susan Fuhrman (1990). "The National Interest and the Federal Role in Education," *Publius: The Journal of Federalism* 20 (Summer).

Ewell, Peter J. (1999). "Assessment of Higher Education Quality: Promise and Politics." In *Assessment in Higher Education: Issues of Access, Quality, Student Development, and Public Pol-*

icy. Samuel J. Messick, ed. Mahwah, NJ: Lawrence Erlbaum Associates, Publishers.

Esping-Anderson, Gosta (1990). *The Three Worlds of Welfare Capitalism.* Princeton: Princeton University Press.

Finn, Chester E. (1984). "Trying Higher Education: An Eight-Count Indictment." *Change* (May/June): 29–33, 47–51.

Fitzpatrick, Ellen F. (1990). *Endless Crusade: Women Social Scientists and Progressive Reform.* New York: Oxford University Press.

Freeland, Richard M. (1992) *Academia's Golden Age: Universities in Massachusetts, 1945–1970.* New York: Oxford University Press.

Freeman, Richard (1971). *The Market for College Trained Manpower.* Cambridge: Harvard University Press.

——— (1975). "Overinvestment in College Training?" *Journal of Human Resources* 10: 287–311.

——— (1976). *The Overeducated American.* New York: Academic Press.

Gallagher, Catherine (1997). "The History of Literary Criticism." *Daedalus* 126 (Winter): 133–153.

Geiger, Roger L. (1986). *To Advance Knowledge: The Growth of American Research Universities, 1900–1940.* New York: Oxford University Press.

——— (1993). *Research and Relevant Knowledge: American Research Universities Since World War II.* New York: Oxford University Press.

——— (1995). "The Era of Multi-Purpose Colleges in American Higher Education, 1850–1890," *History of Higher Education Annual* 15: 51–92.

Glassick, Charles E., Mary Taylor Huber, and Gene I. Maeroff (1997). *Scholarship Assessed: Evaluation of the Professoriate.* An Ernest L. Boyer Project of the Carnegie Foundation for the Advancement of Teaching. San Francisco: Jossey-Bass.

Goldin, Claudia and Lawrence F. Katz (2008). *The Race between Education and Technology.* Cambridge: Harvard University Press.

Gordon, Lynn (1990). *Gender and Higher Education in the Progressive Era.* New Haven: Yale University Press.

Graham, Patricia A. (2005). *Schooling in America.* New York: Oxford University Press.

Grubb, W. Norton (1991). "The Decline of Community College Transfer Rates: Evidence from National Longitudinal Surveys." *Journal of Higher Education* 62, no. 2: 194–217.

———— (1992). "The Economic Returns to Baccalaureate Degrees: New Evidence from the Class of 1972." *The Review of Higher Education* 15 (Winter): 213–231.

———— (1996). *Learning to Work: The Case for Re-integrating Job Training and Education.* New York: Russell Sage.

———— (1996). *Working in the Middle: Strengthening Education and Training for the Mid-Skilled Labor Force.* San Francisco: Jossey-Bass.

———— (2009). *The Money Myth: School Resources, Outcomes, and Equity.* New York: Russell Sage.

Grubb, W. Norton, et. al. (1999). *Honored but Invisible: An Inside Look at Teaching in Community Colleges.* New York: Routledge.

Grubb, W. Norton and Marvin Lazerson (2004). *The Education Gospel: the Economic Power of Schooling.* Cambridge: Harvard University Press.

Grubb, W. Norton and Marvin Lazerson (2010). "The Education Gospel and Vocationalism in U.S. Higher Education: Triumphs, Tribulations, and Cautions for Other Countries" in Antje Barabasch and Felix Rauner, eds., *The Art of Integration: Work and Education in America.* Springer.

Gumport, Patricia (1997). "The United States Country Report: Trends in Higher Education from Massification to Post-Massification." Hiroshima: Six Nation Educational Research Project, Hiroshima University.

Hartog, Jan (2000). "Over-education and Earnings." *Economics of Education Review* 19 (February): 131–147.

Hauptman, Arthur M. (1992). "Quality and Access in Higher Education: The Impossible Dream." *American Higher Education: Purposes, Problems and Public Perceptions.* Queensland, MD: The Aspen Institute.

Hauptman, Arthur M. and Maureen A. McLaughlin (1992). "Is the Goal of College Access Being Met?" in *American Higher Edu-*

cation: Purposes, Problems and Public Perceptions. Queensland, MD: The Aspen Institute.

Hecker, Daniel E. (1992). "Reconciling Conflicting Data on Jobs for College Graduates." *Monthly Labor Review* (July): 3–12.

Hofstadter, Richard and Walter P. Metzger (1995). *The Development of Academic Freedom.* New York: Columbia University Press.

Horowitz, Helen L. (1987). *Campus Life: Undergraduate Cultures from the End of the Eighteenth Century to the Present.* New York: Knopf.

Hutchings, Patricia and Ted Marchese (1990). "Watching Assessment. Questions, Stories, Prospects." *Change* (September/October): 14–38.

Hutchings, Pat and Lee S. Shulman (1999). "The Scholarship of Teaching: New Elaborations, New Developments." *Change* (September/October): 11–15.

Jencks, Christopher and David Riesman (1968). *The Academic Revolution.* Chicago: University of Chicago Press.

Jones, Brian (1984). *Sleepers, Wake! Technology and the Future of Work.* Melbourne: Oxford University Press.

Kimball, Bruce A. (1988). "The Historical and Cultural Dimensions of the Recent Reports." *American Journal of Education* 98: 293–322.

Kirp, David (2003). *Shakespeare, Einstein, and the Bottom Line: The Marketing of Higher Education.* Cambridge: Harvard University Press.

Kreps, David M. (1997). "Economics—The Current Position." *Daedalus* 126 (Winter): 59–85.

Kuhn, Thomas (1962). *The Structure of Scientific Revolutions.* Chicago: University of Chicago Press.

Kwon, Dae-Bong (2001). "Adult Education in Korea." Unpublished paper, College of Education, Korea University, Seoul.

Landau, Robert, Thomas Taylor, and Gavin Wright (1996). *The Mosaic of Economic Growth.* Stanford: Stanford University Press.

Lazerson, Marvin, Ursula Wagener, and Larry Moneta (2000). "Like the Cities They Increasingly Resemble, Colleges Must

Train and Retain Competent Managers." *Chronicle of Higher Education* July 28.

Leslie, J. Bruce (1992). *Gentlemen and Community: The College in the "Age of the University," 1865–1917*. State College: Penn State University Press.

Levin, Henry (1977). "Review of *Ph.D.'s and the Academic Labor Market* by Allan Carter and *The Overeducated American* by Richard Freeman." *Harvard Educational Review* 47 (November): 226–231.

Levine, David (1986). *The American College and the Culture of Aspiration, 1915–1940*. Ithaca: Cornell University Press.

Levine, Lawrence W. (1996). *The Opening of the American Mind: Canons, Culture, and History*. Boston: Beacon Press.

Levy, Frank and Richard J. Murnane (1992). "U.S. Earnings Levels and Earnings Inequality: A Review of Recent Trends and Proposed Explanations." *Journal of Economic Literature* 30 (September):1333–1381.

Light, Richard J. (1960) Harvard Assessment Seminars. *Explorations with Students and Faculty about Teaching, Learning and Student Life*.

——— (2001). *Making the Most of College: Students Speak Their Minds*. Cambridge: Harvard University Press.

Lindblom, Charles E. (1990). *Inquiry and Change: The Troubled Attempt to Understand and Shape Society*. New Haven: Yale University Press.

——— (1997). "Political Science in the 1940s and 1950s." *Daedalus* 126 (Winter): 225–252.

Lindblom, Charles E. and David K. Cohen (1979). *Usable Knowledge*. New Haven: Yale University Press.

Link, William (1995). *William Friday*. Chapel Hill: University of North Carolina.

Linn, Robert L. and Kevin G. Welner, eds. (2007). *Race-Conscious Policies for Assigning Students to Schools: Social Science Research and the Supreme Court Cases*. Washington: National Academy of Education.

Lively, Kit (1995). "Continuing Controversy Over Standards: Florida Eases Rule that Students Pass Test to Become Juniors." *The Chronicle of Higher Education*. June 2.

London, Howard (1978). *The Culture of a Community College.* New York: Praeger.

Marchese, Ted (1999). "Assessment Today—And Tomorrow." *Change* (September/October): 4.

Matei, Livui (2008). *The Knowledge Society as a Practical Utopia and the Rediscovery of Universities in Eu*rope. Doctoral Dissertation, University of Bucharest, Romania.

McPherson, Michael S., William G. Bowen, and Matthew M. Chingos (2009). *Crossing the Finish Line: Completing College at America's Public Universities.* Princeton: Princeton University Press.

National Center for Education Statistics (2002, 2008). *Digest of Education Statistics.* Washington, D.C.

National Center for Postsecondary Improvement (1999). "Revolution or Evolution? Gauging the Impact of Institutional Student Assessment Strategies." The Landscape, in *Change* (September/October): 53–56.

National Commission on Excellence in Education (1983). *A Nation at Risk*: *The Imperative for Educational Reform: A Report to the Nation and the Secretary of Education*, U.S. Department of Education. Washington, D.C.: The Commission.

National Research Council (2003). *Engaging Schools: Fostering High School Students' Motivation to Learn.* Washington, D.C.: National Academies Press.

National Governors' Association Task Force on College Quality (1986). *Time for Results.* Washington, D.C.: National Governors' Association, Center for Policy Research and Analysis.

National Institute of Education (1984). *Involvement in Learning.* Washington, D.C.: National Institute of Education, US Department of Education.

Nehamas, Alexander (1997). "Trends in Recent American Philosophy." *Daedalus* 126 (Winter): 209–223.

New York Review of Books, March 27, 1997.

Newman, Frank (1985). *Higher Education and the American Resurgence.* Princeton, N.J.: Carnegie Foundation for the Advancement of Teaching.

Pascarella, Ernest T. and Patrick T. Terenzini (1991). *How College Affects Students.* San Francisco: Jossey-Bass.

President's Commission on Higher Education (1947). *Higher Education in American Democracy*. New York: Harper.

Rawls, John (1971). *A Theory of Justice*. Cambridge: Harvard University Press.

Reuben, Julie A. (1996). *The Making of the Modern University: Intellectual Transformation and the Marginalization of Morality*. Chicago: University of Chicago Press.

Rudolph, Frederick (1977). *Curriculum: A History of the Undergraduate Course of Study Since 1636*. San Francisco: Jossey-Bass.

Ryan, P. (2001). "The School-to-Work Transition: A Cross-national Perspective. *Journal of Economic Literature* 39(1): 34–92.

Schmidt, Peter (1996). "More States Tie Spending on Colleges to Meeting Specific Goals." *Chronicle of Higher Education*. May 24.

Schorske, Carl E. (1997). "The New Rigorism in the Human Sciences, 1940–1960." *Daedalus* 126 (Winter): 289–309.

Scott, Joan Wallach (1996). "Defending the Tradition of Shared Governance." *Chronicle of Higher Education* (August 9).

Shulman, Lee S. (1987). "Knowledge and Teaching: Foundations of the New Reform." *Harvard Educational Review*. 57, No. 1 (February).

——— (1999). "Taking Learning Seriously." *Change* (July/August).

Sloan, Douglas (1980). "The Teaching of Ethics in the American Undergraduate Curriculum, 1876–1976." In Daniel Callahan and Sissela Bok (eds.), *Ethics Teaching in Higher Education*. New York: Plenum Press.

Smith, Rogers M. (1997). "Still Blowing in the Wind: The American Quest for a Democratic, Scientific Political Science." *Daedalus* 126 (Winter): 253–287.

Solow, Robert M. (1997). "How Did Economics Get That Way and What Way Did It Get?" *Daedalus* 126 (Winter): 39–58.

Survey Research Center, University of Michigan (1965). "What People Think About College." *American Education* (February).

Thelin, John R. (2004). *A History of American Higher Education*. Baltimore: Johns Hopkins University Press.

Tomkins, C. (2002). "Can Art be Taught?" *New Yorker*, April 15, 44–49.

Useem, Michael (1996). *Investor Capitalism: How Money Managers are Changing the Face of Corporate America.* New York: Basic Books.

Van Vught, Frans (2009). *Mapping the Higher Education Landscape: Towards a European Classification of Higher Education.* Springer.

Veblen, Thorstein (1918). *The Higher Learning in America: a Memorandum on the Conduct of Universities by Businessmen.* New York.

Velleneuve, J. (2002). *Composing a Life: Community College Students and Project-Based Learning in a Multimedia Program.* Ph.D. diss., School of Education, University of California, Berkeley.

Wagener, Ursula (1989). "Quality and Equity: The Necessity for Imagination." *Harvard Educational Review* 59 (May): 240–250.

Walzer, Michael (2006). *Just and Unjust Wars: a Moral Argument with Historical Illustrations.* New York: Basic Books.

Wilson, Daniel J. (1990). *Science, Community, and the Transformation of American Philosophy.* Chicago: University of Chicago Press.

Wolf, Alison (2002). *Does Education Matter? Myths About Education and Economic Growth.* London: Penguin Books.

Zemsky, Robert (1997). "Keynote Address: Seminar on Post-Massification." Hiroshima: Six Nation Educational Research Project, Hiroshima University.

Zemsky, Robert (2009). *Making Reform Work: The Case for Transforming American Higher Education.* New Brunswick: Rutgers University Press.

Name Index

Subject Index